DOUBTS ARE NOT ENOUGH

DOUBTS ARE NOT ENOUGH

James A. Simpson

THE SAINT ANDREW PRESS
EDINBURGH

First published in 1982 by
THE SAINT ANDREW PRESS
121 George Street, Edinburgh EH2 4YN

Copyright © James A. Simpson, 1982

ISBN 0 7152 0501 3

Printed in Hong Kong by Permanent Typesetting & Printing Co., Ltd.

Dedication

*To Morag, Neil, Graeme, Alistair, Elaine — and Derick
with affection.*

Other books by James A. Simpson

There is a time to...
Marriage Questions Today

CONTENTS

Oh age that half believest, thou half believest
Half doubtest the substance of thine own half doubt
And half perceivest what thou half perceivest
Standest at thy temple door heart in, head out.

Sidney Lanier

"Remember Peniel, and wrestle with the great themes
even if they throw you."

Dr Russell Maltby
(addressing divinity students)

A MATTER OF CONCERN

A husband and wife, much given to analysing each other, finally decided to separate. "Our shared doubts," said the husband, "were the only things we had in common. They were not enough." It is no different with moral, philosophical and religious doubts. They cannot permanently satisfy.

Christopher Columbus was right to question the geographical theories of his day. But it was not these doubts about a flat earth that made Columbus great. His greatness sprang from his willingness to act on his belief that the earth was round. On the basis of this positive belief he discovered a new world. Centuries before, Abraham and Jesus had refused to believe what everybody else seemed to believe. But as with Columbus, what most set them apart from their contemporaries was not their doubts, but their willingness to act on the basis of what they did believe about God and life.

In our day also there are mistaken beliefs that we ought to doubt. An old hymn says, "Teach me to check the rising doubt, the rebel sigh." That is quite unbiblical. Though the Bible extols faith, it never censors honest doubt. "My hosannas," said Dostoevsky, "have been forged in the crucible of doubt." Many in every age would utter a hearty Amen.

But doubts by themselves are not enough. Only if people are prepared to go on questioning their doubts as well as their beliefs, does doubt lead to stronger faith. It is a matter of concern that so many in our day have settled down in their doubts. They seem quite happy to be professional doubters. They know what they don't believe, but not what they do believe. It is so much easier to doubt and deny than to affirm, to destroy old myths and institutions than to create any living alternatives.

We cannot, however, live a full life or create a new and

1

better world on the basis of shared doubts. We must have some idea what life is for, what its purpose is. When the psychologist William James was asked to write something that might stem the alarming increase in the American suicide rate, he did not write a treatise on self-destruction. Aware that the ultimate enemy in life is not pain or physical hardship, but the feeling that our lives add up to no enduring meaning, he wrote a book entitled, *The Will to Believe*.

When adults attempt to discuss with restless teenagers why they behave the way they do, they often get the reply, "Why not?" Sometimes the young folk mean, "What's to stop me?" but at other times they secretly hope for an answer they can accept. Most thoughtful adolescents want, need and in fact are desperate to believe in something that will make sense out of life and give meaning and significance to it. Some search for this in mind-bending drugs, others in Zen Buddhism, others in astrology, others in anything but their parents' faith!

Karl Marx had justification for describing the kind of religion that was more concerned with ritual than justice, as 'the opium of the people'. This charge could still be levelled against certain Christians and churches, but is it not irreligion which today is the real opiate, the belief that life has no divine origin, meaning or destiny, that we are answerable only to ourselves? That is what drains the energies and enthusiasms, and kills the hopes of people. "What is the use? Nothing ultimately matters." Such a view of life lets a person off from all serious responsibility. If nothing matters, then what he does and what he is does not ultimately matter. Christianity at its noblest, however, far from being an opiate, is a challenging and stimulating faith. The New Testament speaks of 'sound doctrine'. (The Greek literally means 'hygienic teaching'.) When Christianity reflects the mind and compassion of Christ, it is healthy teaching. It ministers to people's deepest needs. It cures them of their self-despisings. Christian faith sheds light on the mystery of life and gives power for the mastery of life.

In his *Letters and Papers from Prison*, Dietrich Bonhoeffer articulated what many still feel. "Surely there has never been a generation in the course of human history with so little ground under its feet as our own." Helmut Thielicke tells of a mother who had been estranged from the Church for several decades. He met her at the bedside of her son who was slowly dying. Dr Thielicke observed how she nursed him with quiet calmness, literally wrapping him in the cloak of her motherliness during his last agonies. She betrayed not a sign of how much she herself was consumed with pain and anxiety. One day Dr Thielicke said to her, "I admire your attitude." Her disconcerting reply was, "Attitude perhaps, but don't look underneath. I haven't a thing to hold on to."

It is my sincere hope that ordinary folk, like that mother, who are perplexed by honest doubts, who are searching for a place to stand and something to hold on to, might be helped by this book to reach a stronger faith and clearer understanding of what it means for daily living that Jesus is "the Way, the Truth and the Life". I hope it will also help interested lay people who are concerned about spiritual values, to think about God, God in Christ, God in history and God in everyday experience.

Sharing G.K. Chesterton's instinctive distrust of the truth of anything that cannot be told in stories or coloured pictures, I have used many illustrations to highlight what I believe are important truths.

My sincere thanks are due to Leonard Scott for his helpful comments and suggestions, and also to my wife, my greatest encourager and critic.

James A. Simpson
Cathedral Manse, Dornoch

CHAPTER ONE

DOUBTS ABOUT GOD

It seems that something has happened that has never happened
before: though we know not just when, or why, or how, or where.
Men have left GOD not for other gods, they say, but for no god.
T.S. Eliot in *Choruses from 'The Rock'*

It is difficult to say where or when it started. But somewhere
along the way Western man began to lose his belief in God as a
vital reality in his life. Many came to regard the idea that God
created man and was the ultimate judge of his actions as out-
dated superstition. At the beginning of this century Julian
Huxley said, "We live in an age when there is neither need nor
room for the supernatural." Many humanists today are
convinced that within a few decades, it will be universally
recognised that faith in God is an anachronism.

"We have no religion. You see my husband is a scientist."
The suburban wife's assumption that atheism is the inevitable
conclusion of any intelligent and scientific mind and that faith in
God is a sure sign of gullibility does not, however, square with
the facts. Whereas the simplicity of Jesus' life and teaching has
attracted many ordinary folk, the profundity of his words, his
personality and his faith have captivated intellectual giants of
the stature of Paul, Michelangelo, Thomas Aquinas, Dietrich
Bonhoeffer and Alexander Solzhenitsyn. The intellectual
difficulties confronting the person who believes that creation is
the product of a divine mind are as nothing compared to the
difficulties confronting the humanist who believes that creation
is the result of sheer accident.

A second assumption of humanism, that things are real
only if you can see them and scientifically analyse or
demonstrate them, is equally mistaken. Are a chemist's
thoughts, which can neither be measured nor perceived, less real

than the chemicals with which he works? Was it not human thought which first liberated the immense power from plutonium? As the writer of the letter to the Hebrews said, the seen is born of the unseen, and the visible of the invisible.

I weigh 69 kg. My wife is 5'1'' tall. These facts can be scientifically verified. But of other facts, such as the fact that we love each other, we are psychologically certain, even though there are no instruments to measure or prove that love.

Balzac's heartless chemist, seeing his wife in tears, exclaims, "Tears. I have analysed tears; tears contain a little phosphate of lime, chloride of sodium, mucus and water." Surely there is more to tears than that! It is no different with beauty. By analysing the chemical composition of the pigments in a painting, a scientist can accurately date it. But when the discussion concerns the all-important question, "Is it a work of art, a thing of beauty?" his precision instruments cannot help.

In a London subway station, a man sprinted along the platform and jumped down on to the track to rescue a girl who had fainted from the path of a fast-approaching train. The materialist might say, "The platform was real, the train was real, but you can only suppose the man's action was good." But those present in that station were more sure that they were watching a brave and good action than of anything else. There are roads to knowledge and certainty other than that of scientific proof. "The heart" as Pascal stated, "has its reasons which the reason knows not of." Most of us would stake our lives on the distinctly unscientific knowledge that our child is of infinite value. Science is one road to truth but not the only road. It does not tell us all there is to know about life and the world. Donald Lowrie wrote:

> The most real things we know are all unreal
> The firmest, truest all intangible.
> Can you weigh mother love as on a scale
> Or with a metre measure loyalty?
> Can you hold solid justice in your hand
> Or with your fingers grasp integrity?

No one can prove by irrefutable logic that God exists, yet for people like Mother Teresa, the blind George Matheson and countless ordinary folk, nothing is more real than the divine love which will not let them go. Life is greatly impoverished when we do not take the invisible into our reckoning. Empty out of the world everything that is not subject to scientific verification and you will have a world in which very few people would want to live. There is so much more to life than what can be touched, tasted, measured, or photographed.

Many humanists have an exceptionally high concept of man. They picture him as basically good and as seriously concerned about truth and social justice. This idea of the 'humaneness of man' is certainly not the result of an unbiassed survey of the human race. Any such survey would show that for every person seriously concerned about truth, many more love truth and falsehood interchangeably, and for every person concerned about justice, more are concerned to ask, 'What's in it for me?'

The humanist portrait of man has been markedly influenced by the Christian understanding of what it means to be truly human. Nevertheless, as it neglects what Christianity also teaches about man's sinfulness and inhumanity, it is a misleading portrait. The humanist who accuses the Christian of making God in his own image, is often guilty of making man in his own image. He is also being more idealistic than scientific in picturing man as one who will respond to rational argument. In every part of the world slick advertising sways mass emotions in directions quite contrary to reason. As Freud pointed out, when the emotions and reason conflict, the emotions almost always win.

'God created the heavens and the earth'. 'At the heart of the universe there is One who loves, cares and forgives'. Such beliefs have their attendant puzzles, but they do at least shed considerable light on the mystery of life. The belief on the other hand that the universe is mindless, that there was no thought behind its creation, has no luminosity whatsoever. In the place of unsolved riddles here and there we are left with a universe which is itself one gigantic riddle. No intelligence foresaw or controlled the gathering of the atoms. No plan lies behind the ebb and flow of the seasons or the story of evolution. The appearance of life in the world was not foreseen or expected. It simply appeared, a chance occurrence. Somehow the mindless process gave birth to mind; the unthinking produced thought. To believe that puts a greater stress on human intelligence than anything the Christian faith asks people to believe. As a rational human being I cannot accept that the mechanics of the human fingers, the wonders of the human eye, the brain of Plato and the heart of Jesus all happened by sheer accident.

Dr John Baillie told how he was happy to count among his friends men and women of high intellectual distinction who had returned to the Christian outlook after years of defection from it. In practically every case the renewed hospitality of their minds to Christian truth came through their awakening to the essential untenability of the alternative position, and to the realisation that the hypothesis of God gives a more reasonable interpretation of the world than any other. Whereas Christianity has its lights and shadows, its illuminations and mysteries, atheism offers only unanswered questions.

"Cease to believe in God and everything is permitted." In saying this, Dostoevsky was not casting aspersions on the morality or integrity of atheists or humanists. Some humanists exhibit every Christian virtue but faith in God. They believe that although Jesus was mistaken in his thinking about God, he was substantially right about how life should be lived. They continue to accept the commandments, "You shall not kill or steal or lie", "You shall love your neighbour as yourself", without believing that they were commanded. Part of the problem about such an ethic without absolutes or sanctities, is that when strongly tempted many instinctively regard such sanctions as less binding. In a remarkably honest statement, Aldous Huxley said that he wondered whether this had not been part of the appeal of atheism in his early days. "Why was I so insistent on a materialistic explanation of everything? Was it because I wanted my freedom to do as I please? I knew that with a materialistic philosophy I had just that. Whereas once I admitted that the spiritual was present in life, I had to listen to something, someone, beyond myself who would put a curb, a demand upon me that I was unwilling to face."

The virtues which many humanists prize are like the Christmas trees we bring into our homes. No matter how much we spray them to prevent the needles from falling, they will eventually fall, simply because the tree has been cut off from its roots. Likewise where there is no belief in God or in ultimate right, moral standards and human ideals are devalued.

The first step in the process is often a loss of morale. The humanist Joseph Krutch said, "There is no reason to suppose that man's own life has any more meaning than the life of the humblest insect." According to Jean Paul Sartre, another distinguished humanist, "The life of the solitary drunkard and the great statesman are equally pointless." Is there enough inspiration in such a view of life to inspire people to concern themselves about the plight of the poor and those discriminated against, to labour and sacrifice for a better world? Would it not be more likely to undermine their idealism and intensify the temptation just to settle for what they can get out of life?

A little girl had worked hard at school making a surprise present for her parents. She had moulded a clay dish, fired it and painted it. She was justifiably proud of it. But as she rushed into her home with it, she tripped and fell. The dish broke with a fearful ceramic crash. Hearing her screams, her parents rushed through from the kitchen. Her father, seeing what had happened, unthinkingly said, "It does not really matter, dear." Fortunately her mother was much wiser. Taking the little girl in her arms she hugged her and said, "It does matter dear. It matters a great deal." There is nothing more demoralising than the feeling that what we do does not count. By contrast, the belief that the little things we do and the way we do them matter vitally to God, that we are fellow-labourers with him in the task of creating a fairer, finer world, has not only undergirded many to persevere when tempted to say, "What's the use?" it has also transformed many a lowly and routine job.

Humanism not only destroys morale. It also destroys the roots of many of the values which humanists cherish. Sartre frankly acknowledged the hollowness of values that are merely the product of social custom. If we believe there is nothing behind this universe but protons and electrons going it blind, that life is no more than a chance occurrence on a very minor planet, then the logical corollary is that our values and standards are purely relative. They have no roots in the process or backing from it, for the process is non-moral. Jesus and Nero,

Schweitzer and Hitler are equally the product of mindless evolution. They do not admit of praise or blame. The universe looks on indifferently.

Suppose a government were to decide on the death penalty for people whose continued existence it found contrary to the welfare of the nation, as the Nazis found the mentally handicapped undesirable. On what basis would we oppose such a decree, short of invoking God's law or appealing to the sacredness of life? If what a government decrees is man's highest law, then we cannot say their actions are morally wrong. Barbara Ward reminds us, "It was as children of God that men received their title to sovereign and inalienable rights. It was as immortal souls that they claimed a unique and equal status. It was in the will of God that they saw enshrined the laws and rights which no government might transgress." When such beliefs are undermined, the tendency is to trim the moral ideals of Mount Sinai and Galilee to the level of what is expedient or economically necessary or acceptable to the bulk of society.

The teenager's plea that 'everybody else is doing it', implying that it is therefore right for him, has in fact in our day been elevated into an adult ethical principle. Since everybody else puts profit before principle, fiddles income-tax returns and 'passes by' on the other side without lending a hand, why should not we? It is significant that the Kinsey report on sexual behaviour was widely interpreted, not just as a statistical assessment of how people actually behave, but as an indication of what is now permissible in the sphere of sexual morality. We have unwittingly moved over to a statistical gallup-poll morality. For a popular fictional hero like James Bond, traditional Christian morality has ceased to exist. He lies, cheats, steals, maims, kills. Every time he goes abroad he commits adultery. Having no faith in God he feels everything is permitted.

Our moral crisis is as much one of belief as of behaviour. Reviving faith in the God in whom Jesus believed and whom he sought to serve will do more to restore Christian standards than passing stricter laws. In so far as humanists seek truth and the well-being of people, and in so far as they stress the importance of social responsibility, they are our natural allies. What we need to do is to enter upon a dialogue in which we strive to show that the ideals cherished by concerned humanists can best be fulfilled when they rest on the Christian understanding of life.

Life, I suppose, can afford a little irreligion here and there, but it cannot afford thorough-going atheism, the loss of faith in the underlying friendliness of the world we live in, or the loss of trust in the essential goodness and meaningfulness of life.

CHAPTER TWO

DOUBTS ABOUT BELIEF

"If I can do anyone a good turn, that is going to be my religion."

"It does not really matter whether a person is a Christian or an atheist, so long as he is kind and good."

Many feel certain that what a person believes is of no great moment. It is doing what is right that matters. Such a liberal outlook sounds attractive, but how full of inaccuracies and over-simplifications it is! What is right? What is good?

An electric saw is a good saw when it cuts wood well. It was made for that purpose. A man is a good man when he does what well? For what purpose was he created? Some would reply, "A man is a good man when he leads a decent life." But what is a decent life? Why not lie if by doing so we can make a profit? Why not seek revenge on those who wrong us? Why care for the elderly? Only what a person believes about the meaning and purpose of life can enable him to answer such basic questions.

We are all in the business of believing. The world in which we live is a battlefield of contending faiths. Some believe in a democratic form of government, others in a totalitarian form. Some believe in comprehensive education, others in selective education. Some believe abortion should be available on demand, others that it should be available only if the mother's health is at risk. Some believe in a divided Ireland, others in a united Ireland. Some believe in the God Jesus Christ believed in, some in the God Mohammed worshipped, others do not believe in God at all.

The history of believing is an endless series of illustrations of the importance of people's convictions. It was because the ancient Egyptians believed that Pharoah was divine that they accepted without question his use of the national resources to gratify his desires. It was because the people of ancient Ur believed that when the king died he passed into another realm, that they buried his wife and servants alive with him. It was because the Roman Church hierarchy believed at the time of the Inquisition that heresy was the worst of crimes, treason against Almighty God, that they made the punishment more severe than for any other crime. It is because the communists believe they have a creed worth sharing that they pour their propaganda by the ton into the newly literate countries. With such illustrations in mind, it is difficult to understand how many in the West are of the opinion that it does not really matter what people believe.

There are two main reasons for the prevalence of this mistaken idea. In the first place it is common today to find people who have completely different beliefs about God, acting in almost the same way, treating people in the same way and having almost identical standards. One finds Christians and atheists fighting to uphold the dignity of man, caring for the underprivileged and the oppressed. But one also finds professing Christians and atheists whose prime concern is self-advancement and self-glorification. The closing sentence of the obituary notice of a city businessman surprised two of his colleagues. "The funeral service will be held in the Methodist church where for many years Mr — was a member." It prompted the comment, "Well he is the last person I would have thought of as a churchman." According to the artificial classifications which categorise people as Jews, Christians, Muslims or atheists, the deceased bore the name Christian, but apparently he had seldom based his words or actions on the faith he professed. There being many Christians with such a non-committal belief in God, it is not surprising that they are not noticeably different from non-Christians.

The difference is further minimised by the fact that many of our everyday assumptions are a legacy from the Christian faith of our parents and grandparents. The long accumulated effect of Christian teachings, mediated through our literature, family traditions and social customs, has become part and parcel of the mentality of many in the West, even of those who think of themselves as atheists. There is for example the widespread acceptance, at least in theory, that the strong should help the weak, that the individual is precious, that the truly great are the

'Good Samaritans' who lend a helping hand, who go the second mile. Virtues like forgiveness, humility, compassion, chastity were given their pre-eminence by the Christian Church.

In the world of Jesus' day, a world founded on military might and slavery, there was little or no bad conscience among the slave owners about war, slavery or poverty, or among mothers about abandoning their children almost as soon as they were born, especially if they were girls. In the Epistle to Diognetus, written as late as the third century, we read, "Christians marry and bear children as others do, but they do not expose their children." The discarding of children was obviously still widespread in the third century. In the ancient world there was also little bad conscience among the Jews about their prejudices against the Samaritans and Romans.

If people were to ask themselves why they believe many of the things they do, and why they hold to certain standards, they would probably discover that it was because their forefathers believed that Christ who taught these things did in fact reveal the truth about life. The transformation of many of the assumptions upon which life is lived has taken place under the influence of the Christian Gospel.

For these two reasons, that many associated with the Church do not practise what they profess and that many outside the Church live on the ethical capital of their Christian forebears, there appears on the surface to be evidence to support the theory that as far as conduct is concerned, it does not matter what a person believes.

We must however clearly distinguish between what a person professes to believe and what he really does believe. The latter is best ascertained from the assumptions on which he acts daily. His diary and cheque book stubs often reveal more about his beliefs than the hymns he sings or the creed he recites in church. When we are brought into close contact with death, when we are personally wronged, or when an immigrant family moves in next door, our reactions reveal more about what we really believe about death, forgiveness and the brotherhood of man, than anything we say in study groups.

Studdert Kennedy tells of a man who regularly professed his faith in God the Father Almighty and in the Holy Spirit. But his real creed went more like this: "I believe in Alcohol Almighty, Lord of all good living, bestower of true peace. I believe in the fiery spirit that can give the coward courage and make the dumb man speak, that soothes all sorrows, dries all tears and gives the weary rest." In the hour of crisis it was to the bottle that he instinctively turned.

The god we really worship is whoever or whatever is our ultimate concern. Should someone overhear our secret thoughts and desires, would they hear a prayer that we might fulfil the purpose for which God created us, or would they hear a prayer that we might become more popular or prosperous? Or what would they hear? What is our ultimate concern? Paul could say in effect, "Life means Christ to me." If they were to be honest, some people would say, "Life means power to me, or promotion or wealth, or football or golf." Things that have a rightful secondary place are allowed to creep up on to the throne of life.

A person's true god is whoever or whatever he adores secretly. The worship of such a god markedly affects our lives. It determines the kind of person we will become. With the alcoholic everything is determined by drink. All his actions and strivings are directed to that end. It is the same with the man whose unadmitted god is money or bridge. His whole timetable is arranged round this god of his creating. The worship of such a god moulds him as a person, for what he deems of ultimate importance determines to a marked degree his priorities and how he lives his life. Although it does not matter what a person professes to believe, it does matter vitally what he does believe in his heart of hearts.

Modern inventions, innoculations which immunise from disease, a synthesis of chemicals which yields a new dye or plastic, the structure of a helicopter or supersonic aircraft, all depend on correct interpretations of the substances and forces of which our world is built. Correct beliefs about the physical world are important. So too are correct beliefs about the nature and purpose of life. It makes a difference whether a person believes he is called by God to use his talents in the interests of the great human family, or whether he believes that life and the universe are without divine origin or moral purpose. It also ultimately makes a difference whether we believe that justice, mercy, truth and love matter above all else because they are reflections of divine characteristics, or whether we believe that there is no rhyme or reason anywhere.

The Nazi philosopher Rosenberg believed that the lesson of history was that although numerous races had inhabited this world, only the Germans had produced anything of value. The contribution of the others to art, science, music, civilisation and culture generally had been minimal. The contribution of the Jews he regarded as positively evil. Accept these beliefs and all the various steps in Hitler's theory and practice follow with a logic as relentless as the march of his goose-stepping legions. Convinced that everything good in life had been produced by the German race, Hitler felt justified in attempting to treble the population of Germany by encouraging illegitimacy. He felt justified too in seeking to extend Germany's frontiers to obtain more room for the expansion of the master race. Since the contribution of the Jews to civilisation had been positively evil, he felt justified in getting Eichmann to exterminate these 'pests' by the millions, just as British farmers have on occasions exterminated rabbits. Hitler's terrifying beliefs, the substitution of the Fatherland for Almighty God, himself for the Divine Son and the spirit of German Nationalism for the Holy Spirit, became the parents of scores of fearful actions. They plunged the world into a war that cost millions of lives.

According to modern reasoning the Nazis had as much right to their beliefs as we have to ours. We may find such beliefs detestable, but by the same token the Nazis did not like what we believed. Hitler called the Sermon on the Mount an ethic for cowards and idiots. If we rule out the idea that there is ultimate truth about what human conduct ought to be, we are not entitled to say that Nazi beliefs were wrong. When we use the word 'wrong' we are referring to an ultimate standard by which all beliefs are to be judged.

A modern poet says,

> How can we say this is bad, this is good,
> When we know nothing about it, having no standards
> Nor faith to judge by? Like flies in a vacuum.

Either we are animals.... clever in some ways,
Degenerate in others and follow instinct,
Or else we are something else and ought to do otherwise.

I wish to God I had some religion.

The English biologist Thomas Huxley rightly said, ''The longer I live the more obvious it is to me that the most sacred act of a man's life is to say and feel 'I believe'.'' For society, as well as for the individual, a set of beliefs is no mere decorative fringe, but a central basic necessity.

CHAPTER THREE

DOUBTS ABOUT THE BIBLE
(1)

My attention was recently drawn to an advert in the 'For Sale' column of *The Falkirk Herald.* "Black goatskin covered bible with zip, very good condition. Never been read. £5." Writing in *The Sunday Times*, Michael Parkinson told how during an autographing session in a Manchester bookshop, he noticed that the Bible which one lady gave him to sign had just been newly purchased. He asked her why she had chosen the Bible. "Oh I just looked around for something I had not read."

Despite the fact millions of Bibles are sold every year, and that the Bible can now be read in simple contemporary English, Protestants today are probably more ignorant of its contents and central characters than at any other time in the history of Protestantism. Michael Parkinson, Mohammed Ali and Margaret Thatcher we know well, but who are Amos of Tekoa, John of Patmos or Mary of Magdala? When people loudly protest that 'the Protestant Church stands on the Word of God', I am sometimes tempted to reply, "I wish her members would take it out from under their feet and read it."

Some speak of the Bible in glowing terms as great literature, suggesting that it is on a par with Shakespeare. In one sense they are right. The King James Version is a magnificent example of English prose, and yet that is emphatically *not* the reason why Christians regard the Bible as the most important book in the world. To read the Bible simply as great literature would be, as someone said, like reading Moby Dick as a whaling manual.

Others use the phrase 'the Good Book' to highlight their belief that the Bible is the supreme rule book of the good life, an everyman's guide to good conduct. There is some truth in this. The commandments and many of the moral maxims of the Book of Proverbs are very relevant in our world where dishonesty, delinquency, idolatry and killing are uncomfortably common. The social conscience of the 20th century still lags far behind that of the Jewish prophets. By common consent the Sermon on the Mount is the noblest utterance on the moral life to be found anywhere. Yet despite this, if we think of the Bible's uniqueness or greatness primarily in terms of a guide book for decent living, or a gauge to test the defects of society, we are going to find ourselves in trouble. "Noah got drunk. Why shouldn't I?" was the adolescent's question. In the Bible you find laws which forbid shaving and cutting hair. "Do not cut the hair on the sides of your head or trim your beard." (Lev. 19:27) In its pages you find laws which would make even a militant Zionist blush, like the one that says that Israel is totally to destroy conquered peoples, showing no mercy. There is also advice on how to handle a delinquent child which even the strictest of modern parents would hesitate to accept. In the book of Deuteronomy we are told to drag such a child before the local magistrates and stone him to death. "You will thus rid yourselves of this wickedness." (Deut. 21:21 N.E.B.)

If the Bible is not primarily a rule book for the good life, what is it? Some say it is a book about ourselves. Again there is considerable truth in this. In its pages we meet the kind of people who walk our streets, crusaders and crooks, heroes and saints with feet of clay, people living in the quiet assurance of faith and painfully groping their way through the unanswered 'whys' of life, people who joyfully affirm the presence of God and at other times agonise over the silence of God. The Bible does not mention the green pound, or space-flights. It is not even aware that our earth is a planet in the solar system. But it does speak about you and me.

On the cover of a child's trick book were the words, "Wild animals I have known". Inside there were no animal pictures, only a mirror and the reflection of the reader! The Bible is rather like that. At first it seems a simple story of men and women long ago. But within its pages we see ourselves, our rebellion, pride, deep longing for meaning and God. Some feel a kinship with Moses, shrinking from the responsibilities of leadership and with Elijah and Jeremiah, at times despondent under the pressure of hostile opposition, yet at other times facing danger with great courage. How often we are like Pilate, washing our hands of difficult problems. How often like Peter we are proud to be associated with Jesus when among his followers, yet reticent when among those who have no time for Jesus. Do we not see ourselves in the promise-making, promise-breaking Peter? The Biblical situation is our situation. The Bible does help us better to understand ourselves, by telling us things about ourselves we did not know before.

Every day we are involved with questions about things that matter a good deal at the time, but scarcely at all the following week. At the same time we tend to pay little attention to questions about things that matter always, life and death questions about meaning, purpose and value. "What shall it profit a man if he gain the whole world and forfeit his own life?" "What does a man gain by all the toil at which he toils?" "If a man die, shall he live again?" "What shall I do to inherit eternal life?" "Who is my neighbour?" "What is truth?" The Bible keeps reminding us of these basic questions.

This is, however, still not the reason why the Protestant Church holds the Bible in such high regard. The uniqueness and greatness of the Bible lies in the fact that it is a book about God and the purposes of God. The Bible is more interested in interpreting events than in communicating historical and biographical facts. The authors of the various books select and narrate particular events with one object in mind, to demonstrate the purposes of God in history. In the Bible the inmost heart of Almighty God is laid bare. Men like Hosea, Isaiah and Moses were sufficiently sensitive to his presence to be able to glimpse truths about God and life for their time, truths big enough to be valid for all time. The Bible is the record of God's dealings with people at certain supremely significant times. In order that we might know him more clearly, love him more dearly and follow him more nearly, God "in the fulness of time" sent Jesus into the world. In the life of Jesus of Nazareth, God revealed himself as fully as was possible through a man in the days of the Roman Empire. What power this record has to speak to us today, to deepen our awareness of God and our understanding of the wisdom, love and power behind all created things!

Those who turn to the Bible in times of crisis, are not concerned about whether it is great prose or poetry. Made suddenly aware of the brief and uncertain lease they or their loved ones have on life, they hunger for the assurance that life is meaningful and that the God who made this world and all things in it is not indifferent to what happens to us. The Bible provides these assurances. It reminds us of the eternal dimension to life. It reminds us also that at the helm there is a caring hand, that God in character is like Jesus, caring as Jesus cared, forgiving as Jesus forgave. This is the 'Good News' of the Bible.

If we look *at* a car window, we will often see dirt and dead insects. But if we look *through* the window we will see the world beyond. Something like that is the difference between those who constantly look for the flaws and contradictions in the Bible, and those who see past the flaws to the divine light which the Bible sheds on the mystery of life and eternal things.

G.K. Chesterton once remarked that a number of his contemporaries seemed to be labouring under the delusion that they had read Darwin's '*The Origin of Species*' and were therefore well qualified to pronounce that men are descended from monkeys or else dogmatically to dismiss the theory. It is no different with the Bible. Many who speak for or against it have never made time to read it.

When the editorial committee of the Penguin Classics Series decided to make a new 'unbiassed' translation of the four gospels, they asked E.V. Rieu who was an agnostic to undertake the work. On hearing of this, a friend of E.V. Rieu's said to his son, "I wonder what your father will do to the Gospels!" "I wonder," replied the son, who was a practising Christian, "what the Gospels will do to my father." To translate the four Gospels his father had to study them in depth. As his son suspected, this had a profound effect on him. He found Christ in the Bible and new life in him. In the introduction to his translation, he wrote:

> Of what I have learned from these documents in the course of my task, I will say only this, that they bear the seal of the Son of Man and God. They are the Magna Charta of the human spirit. Were we to devote to their comprehension a little of the selfless enthusiasm that is now expended on the riddle of our physical surroundings, we

should cease to say that Christianity is coming to an end. We might even feel it had only just begun.

To those who would study the Bible, I would say the following things.

Begin with a modern translation. The literary style may not compare with the King James Version, but the message is clearer, and surely it is the message which is of prime importance.

Remember that the Bible is a library of books of varied types. The sixty-six books in the library were written for a variety of purposes, by many varied hands over a period of almost two thousand years. Each book has therefore to be studied differently. It is of no use trying to read poetry or drama as though it were sober, factual history. It is of no use addressing to a hymn the kind of questions we would ask of a scientific theory.

Remember that history in the Bible is seen through the eyes of a believer in God. The Old Testament 'history' books are really 'theological history' books in which the hero is God, not the Jewish nation. This explains why so many unflattering incidents in the life of the Jewish nation are frankly reported. Whereas most national histories are written to show the nation in a good light, the Old Testament historians were chiefly concerned to remind their contemporaries of the amazing grace and patience of God.

When reading the great 'faith-stories' in the Bible, like those of Adam and Eve, the Tower of Babel and Jonah, remember that whereas we immediately ask, "Did this actually happen?" the concern of the oriental man from whose environment these stories came, was "What is the message in these stories?" The oriental mind thought in pictures and expressed itself in non-philosophical language. The oriental embodied his teaching in stories, whether parable or seeming historical narrative. The last thing he would think to ask would be whether the selected persons, events and circumstances which so vividly illustrated his teaching were in themselves real or fictitious. The writers of the early chapters of Genesis, for example, were no more concerned with anthropological, astronomical or geological facts than Robert Burns was concerned with botany when he wrote, "My love is like a red, red rose". Their concern was with ultimate questions. What was God's purpose in creation? What ought to be man's relationship to God? What has gone wrong with the human situation? In answering these questions, they used language of such symbolic imagery that even the non-intellectual could understand. Of the Genesis story of Cain and Abel, John Steinbeck wrote, "This one story is the basis of all human neurosis—and if you take the fall along with it, you have the total of the psychic troubles that can happen to a human." To make Adam or Cain historical people, or to literalise a talking serpent, obscures the tremendous message of the early chapters of Genesis. Another dramatist has said of man, "Give him an Eden and he straightway loses it, a garden and he turns it into a quagmire, a dream and it becomes a nightmare, a prophet and he is stoned into a corpse." The story of Genesis 1-11 is the story of Mr and Mrs Everyman.

Read selectively. Many have come to grief by starting at Genesis and ploughing their way through Exodus, Leviticus and Numbers. There are books in the Biblical library, large parts of which are extremely dull, like the six long chapters in Exodus that describe the Temple and its workings, right down to the composition of the curtains. There are other parts which are difficult to understand. Jerome, the distinguished Biblical scholar of the 4th century compared the study of Ezekiel to walking through the catacombs where light seldom breaks through. John Calvin never finished his commentary on Ezekiel. He gave up! Someone once likened reading the Bible to eating fish. The bones you cannot digest you put to one side and you eat what you can. When you start reading the Bible, start with the more easily digested parts. In the 'bones' or the 'dry valleys' you may later discover much that is of considerable worth, but don't start there. Start with one of the gospels, possibly Mark's, and learn all you can about the life and teaching of Jesus.

In the garden of Hampton Court there is a network of intricately laid out paths and hedges. Many get lost in the maze. The problem of finding one's way through the maze is greater today than in previous years, for no longer is there a royal guard positioned on a high platform overlooking the scene. Formerly it was possible to take your bearings from him and thus find your way through the maze. This applies also to the Bible. At times it seems like a great maze. If we are not to get lost we will have to take our bearings from Christ. He corrects what is misleading and mistaken in other parts of the Bible. He clarifies much that is not clear, and fulfils all that is gloriously right.

Use a good commentary. This will provide the necessary background material. It will explain what special circumstances caused a certain book to be written. For the New Testament it is doubtful if there are any better commentaries for lay people than those by Dr William Barclay. Not surprisingly millions of copies have already been sold. Dr Barclay probably did more than anyone to make the Bible come alive for modern man, to relate the Biblical message to present-day life.

One of the saddest things about our world is the number of people who drift aimlessly from youth to age. For them man seems to be just an eddy of purposeless dust in a vast universe. What we call history they see as just 'one darned thing after another'. It was not always so. For our forefathers, nurtured as many of them were on the Bible, life had great horizons.

> Life is real! Life is earnest!
> And the grave is not its goal.

I am certain we will never restore such a sense of purpose and destiny to people's lives until the Bible becomes, not just the book of the clergy or the book that is read in church, but the book of the people.

CHAPTER FOUR

DOUBTS ABOUT THE BIBLE
(2)

"Literary classics are books which everyone has heard about, but which few have actually read." There is considerable truth in that remark. Many well educated people are unfamiliar with the writings of Shakespeare and Dickens, Camus and Solzhenitzen. They are widely read, but more in the sphere of newspapers and textbooks than in the sphere of great literature. Their main aim in reading is to acquire the facts they seek.

We miss, however, the wonder of great literature if we approach it with this intention. In plays and poems facts are secondary. Of prime importance is the author's mind. It is with this that we seek to make personal contact.

An ever-increasing proportion of what is written in our time consists of brief newspaper reports, White Papers, technical journals and other literature of the textbook kind in which it is the information contained that is of prime importance. That being so it is not surprising that there has grown up a widespread impatience with poetry, drama and philosophy. During four years of science studies at the University, I read very little general literature. The result was that I almost lost the technique of making contact in a book with another mind at a deep level.

One of the obstacles in the way of people understanding the Bible is this prevalent impatience with poetic language and with literature that does not state everything plainly. Literal-minded Westerners prefer the language of science and logic where words are defined with greater precision, where a lion is always a large carnivorous animal, and not as in the writings of Jeremiah, a military enemy. Poetry is extravagant with hyperbole and metaphor. Its connections are emotional rather than logical. Although poetic language lacks precision and simplicity, it penetrates to depths that logic cannot reach. Life is not always simple. Its profoundest truths can be communicated only through literature that will yield none of its treasures to the impatient. The Bible, like Shakespeare's plays, makes considerable demands on its readers, but its rewards are also great. Through its pages we communicate with other minds at a deep level and learn from their insights.

In speaking of God and his dealings with people, the Biblical writers do not use the bald language of science or logic, but poetic and symbolic language. All human language falls short of describing God as he actually is, the language of philosophical abstraction no less than that of poetic image. The best we can do is to erect certain signposts which point towards the nature of God. In both the Old and New Testaments the greatest passages concerning God are suffused with a sense of mystery, with the knowledge that there is depth beyond depth in the divine nature which we will never comprehend. It is the most confident believers who humbly acknowledge their limited insight into what Paul called ''the deep things of God'', who say with Isaiah, ''There is no searching of his understanding.''

It is unfair to single out the Christian faith as a target for criticism because it uses poetic rather than scientific language, symbols rather than formulae, for unwittingly we all constantly use metaphors in everyday conversation. No one blames a mother for saying her daughter was 'green with envy' or came home 'in a flood of tears' and 'sank into her arms'. No one blames the economist for speaking of 'frozen assets' or 'floating the pound'. Nobody criticises the chairman for speaking of a committee member as a 'pain in the neck' or the town-planner for talking of a 'bottle-neck' or a 'concrete jungle'. Not one of these phrases is literally true, yet they help communicate an idea which is readily understood by the man in the street. Since we accept hundreds of such usages in everyday speech and writing, why should we insist that expressions such as ''the voice of God'', or ''seated at the right hand of God the Father'' or ''tongues like flames of fire'' must either be literally true or totally false. They are neither. When John the Baptist speaks of Jesus as ''the Lamb of God'', and when Jesus says of himself, ''I am the door'', we take what they say seriously, but not literally.

Personality is the highest idea our minds can encompass, the loftiest product of the world's evolution. Until men think of a higher concept, the Church will continue to think of God, not as a 'person' in any man-sized sense, but as one with whom we can have personal dealings, one whom Jesus spoke of as "our Father". God has more in common with persons than with any other reality we can imagine or describe. He may be beyond personality; he is certainly not less. He is not just some kind of impersonal creative force. God as friend, God as father, God as shepherd, are three of the phrases or metaphors we use to speak as meaningfully as we can about things unseen and eternal. It is significant that whereas I have never been asked at a funeral to read from the Epistle to the Hebrews, which is a logical master-piece, mourners have often asked me to read the Twenty-third Psalm, which is full of metaphors. "The Lord is my shepherd..." Symbolism is the gateway to the human imagination.

In the Bible we read of the "Spirit of God," "the Holy Spirit". The word spirit originally meant wind. This was true in many different languages, including Latin from which our English word 'spirit' is derived, and German from which the word 'ghost' comes. In both these languages as in other languages, the word for wind ultimately became a metaphor for breath. Then over a period of centuries the word for breath came to suggest not just the air that fills the lungs, but the soul or the personality. Those who have watched while a person was dying will understand how natural it was to link breath and the animating power of life itself.

When the Authorised Version of the Bible was translated, the words 'ghost' and 'spirit' both meant personality. The word 'ghost' has greatly suffered through being loaded with superstitious connotations. The word 'spirit' has suffered too, but not as much. One can still helpfully compare the presence of God to the air we breathe, the air which surrounds us and works life within us, but which we often take for granted. In the same way God sustains us day by day though we often do not recognise the source of this inner strengthening. God is always present, quietly seeking to enlarge our lives. "In him we live, and move, and have our being" (Acts 17:28).

The Bible is filled with other metaphors which suggest the same glorious reality, metaphors like the "hand of God", the "finger of God", the "arm of God". The Psalmist says, "Thou dost beset me behind and before, and layest thy hand upon me." Moses says, "The Lord delivered unto me two tablets of stone, written with the finger of God." The hand and finger of God bear no physical resemblance to the hand and fingers at the end of our arms, not even fingers a thousand miles long! When the writer of Exodus tells us that the commandments were written by the finger of God, he was not, as the film producer Cecil B. De Mille seemed to think, concerned with the physical act of engraving the commandments on stone. His concern was with their source, which he says is God.

Just as many compassionate human actions are performed with the hands, and just as delicate precise work is done by the human fingers, so the compassion and creative ability of God may be suggested by metaphors such as the hand and fingers of God. "Underneath are the everlasting arms." This is certainly symbolic language, but how better to elucidate and mediate the comfort of God, for instance, to a person about to undergo surgery? The Biblical writers also use impersonal metaphors to describe God — refuge, fortress, rock, high tower. The significance of the 'fortress' or 'high tower' does not lie with what they are made of, but with what they do. They protect. Rock can be relied on. Frequently the Spirit of God is depicted in terms of water in its threefold function of quenching thirst, bringing fertility and cleansing.

The person who tries to speak of God and the relation of Jesus to God faces a dilemma. He can attempt to use precise language which very often is unintelligible to the man in the street, or he can use picture language which is intelligible, but not precise. The technical language of theology can be off-putting to the layman. A cartoon going the rounds shows Jesus talking to his disciples. He asks them, "Who do you say that I am?" Simon Peter replies, "You are the eschatological manifestation of the ground of our being." Jesus says, "What?"

The inspired Biblical writers faced this dilemma squarely. Speaking with the tongues of angels was an impossibility. They could speak about the mysteries of existence only with the tongues of men. They therefore decided in favour of poetic, picturesque and imaginative language. As there is no non-human or holy language in which to describe God, they knew their descriptions would be inadequate. But they need not be inappropriate, because the unseen God had drawn close to them and addressed them in men like Moses, Jeremiah, Hosea, and he had disclosed himself supremely in a human life, that of Jesus of Nazareth, the One who finally justifies human speech about God.

Human language is inadequate as a vehicle for describing God. It is also inadequate for describing great spiritual experience. Paul says, ''I know a man in Christ who fourteen years ago was caught up to the third heaven — whether in the body or out of the body I do not know, God knows. And I know that this man was caught up into Paradise...'' (2 Cor. 12:2ff). What a struggle Paul had to describe the indescribable, to relate what had happened in an unforgettable encounter with God. He writes also of the ''length, breadth and height'' of God's love. These are space-time words, yet he had to use them. They were the only terms he possessed to describe the magnitude of a love that goes beyond our comprehending. The Biblical story of Jacob at the ford of Jabbok is a strange passage, again an attempt to describe the indescribable, the internal struggle of a man to whom God has suddenly become real. At first it seems like Esau with whom Jacob is wrestling, Esau the brother whom he had so shamefully treated. At other times it seems like a wrestling between his higher and lower selves. But deeper than all this, it is a wrestling with God.

Sometimes modern critics sound as if they are saying that such bewildering language is all a mistake that could have been avoided if only Paul, or the writer of Genesis, had taken pains to express himself more precisely. We might at least pay these men the compliment of noticing that they can on other occasions write with the greatest possible clarity. In speaking of the really deep things of life the poet and dramatist often get nearer the truth than the theologian.

Human language is also inadequate to describe life after death. Again the Biblical metaphors and picture language are not to be taken literally. The writer of the Book of the

Revelation, being an oriental, did not think in abstract terms like perfect government, perfect service, perfect sinlessness. An artist with words, he describes heaven by saying, ''there shall be no more curse, but the throne of God and the Lamb shall be in it; and his servants shall serve him and they shall see his face.'' A prisoner for his faith on the island of Patmos, John was cut off by the sea from all that he knew and loved best. In heaven, he said, there would be no more sea. There he would not be cut off from the people he loved.

On some of the old plantations in the Southern States of America, one can still see a few of the old slave cabins to which the slaves would return at the end of the day with bruised, bare feet. They are so unbelievably cramped and primitive that it is difficult to believe that they were ever the 'home' of a family of human beings. What a shadow slavery cast over many lives! The slaves had no rights and status. It was in protest against such confinement, poverty and tyranny that the negro spirituals arose. Thus imprisoned, the negro dreamed of the time when he would have shoes, when he would be free. ''When I go to heaven, gonna put on my shoes, gonna walk all over God's heaven.'' Take that literally and it is meaningless. Take it metaphorically and it is full of meaning.

From first page to last, the Bible is packed with metaphors, all of which attempt to describe the indescribable, to speak of things unseen in terms of things that can be seen and understood. We misrepresent the Bible if we take these metaphors and word-pictures literally. We also misrepresent the Bible if we do not take them seriously.

CHAPTER FIVE

DOUBTS ABOUT THE DIVINITY OF JESUS

Emerson said of Jesus, "His name is not so much written as ploughed into the history of the world." H.G. Wells said, "His is easily the dominant figure in history." In his name millions have bowed in homage and regulated their daily lives. Because they believed in him and the things for which he stood, many have been prepared to make great sacrifices. Because of him, great art was born and imperishable literature, poetry and music produced.

This is quite astounding considering the third-rate country in which Jesus lived, the poverty of it all, the slim chance he had, the few years he lived. Yet both within and outwith the Church many would echo H.G. Wells' words. They believe that Jesus was the finest person who ever lived, the model of perfection. It is not the nobility of his manhood that they question, but the other claim that Christians make for Jesus—his divinity.

Many church members are not quite sure what they mean when they speak of Jesus as divine. Many outside the Church who shake their heads and say they don't believe in his divinity are often not quite sure what they are disbelieving. Whatever the divinity of Jesus means, it certainly does not mean that Jesus was not fully human. He was not a 'pretend' man. Nor was he a psychological monstrosity with two minds and two wills, a human one and a divine one. He did not switch humanity and divinity on and off according to the requirements of the moment. The Gospels stress again and again that Jesus was a real man who experienced like the rest of us weariness, thirst, pleasure, suffering and finally death.

What are we to make of this most influential life? Some believe it was an accident, the chance product of blind forces. They believe that Jesus just happened. Others believe that the early disciples were on the trail of everlasting truth when after the resurrection they saw in the life, words and actions of Jesus the visible expression of the mind and heart of God.

When men first picked up magnetised iron, they were faced with a problem. What was this extra quality which made iron exercise a potency which ordinary iron did not possess? Was this extra just a chance happening, or was it a revelation of something profound in the constitution of the world? It was much the same when Madame Curie discovered a metal ore that seemed to be different from any other ore she had previously analysed, in that, for instance, it fogged photographic plates placed near it. Again it turned out to be, not an accident, but a revelation of forces previously unknown.

We cannot avoid such questions about magnetised iron and pitchblende, nor can we avoid them about the unique quality of the life of Jesus. Many who came face to face with him felt awed in his presence. Here obviously was a man of God who lived totally for God, whose belief in God determined all he said and did. His whole life was lived, his work done, his sorrows borne, his temptations faced in the spirit of childlike dependence on one whom he called 'Abba', Father.

There grew in some of his contemporaries a strange sense of his rightful authority over their lives. They were certain they were in the presence of one who was nearer to God than anyone they had ever seen or met, one who had the wisdom of God on his lips and the love of God in his hands.

After the resurrection the apostles went out into the Roman Empire bearing the thrilling message that the unseen God who had created this world at the beginning of time had in the life of Jesus of Nazareth chosen to reveal himself in the clothes and language of mortality. They were now certain that in Jesus they had been confronted with nothing less than the activity of God. In the light of Jesus' death and resurrection they saw everything differently. How blind they had previously been! How slow to believe! The resurrection had opened their eyes to what Jesus had been about from his first coming among them. Convinced now that God had been in Christ, they put themselves unconditionally at his service.

The events of which the apostles spoke and later wrote, the

birth, life, death and resurrection of Jesus, were, they believed, parallel in importance only to the creation of the world. Jesus was not only the centre of their existence, giving it meaning. His coming was also the pivotal point of history, giving it meaning.

In every age since, and not least in our own, many on hearing and reading the gospel records of the life of Jesus, have found themselves gripped by Jesus. He not only stands out from the record with remarkable clarity, but reaches forth from that record asking for the devotion of their hearts, minds, souls and strength, asking to be allowed to shape their lives in accord with that which matters most. "Follow me and I will make you..." Malcolm Muggeridge, an eminent agnostic of the 1950's, entitled a book which he wrote in the 1970's *Jesus — The man who lives*. Speaking at Coventry Cathedral Lord Hailsham said,

> For more than thirty years, Christ has been the light of my life. Many times have I betrayed, neglected, denied the light. But never has the light deserted or betrayed me. Of course I think of Christ as an historical character born and died two thousand years ago. Of course I look for guidance and knowledge about him in the Gospels, in the historical context of the ancient world, in the tradition of the Christian community. But more and more I have come to realise that this is not the essence of what I mean when I say, I believe in Christ. I think of him as alive. I think of him as here and present.

The experience of two other distinguished intellectuals, C.S. Lewis and E.V. Rieu, was similar. Getting to grips with the gospel records changed the course of their lives. For Bonhoeffer the brillant young German theologian who was finally put to death for his avowed opposition to Hitler and Nazism, knowing and serving Jesus were all that mattered.

Where Christians in all ages have found most difficulty has been in verbalising their belief in Jesus, in expressing in human language what they believe about his relationship with God. They have felt constrained to speak of this great mystery, but what words are adequate? When Michelangelo visited the studio of the young Raphael, he saw on the easel a portrait of Christ that Raphael was painting. As the young painter was absent, Michelangelo took his brush and wrote, *Amplius* — Larger. In an attempt to do justice to what they believed about Jesus, the early Christians naturally used the largest and most exalted terms of their culture – 'Son of Man,' 'Son of the Most High,' 'Son of God,' 'Christ,' 'Messiah,' 'Light of the World,' 'Second Adam'... The one through whom they had trans-formingly encountered God and had experienced new life, power and purpose was too big for any one metaphor to do justice to him.

In using such exalted phrases and titles they were not assuming the role of theological professors propounding new and difficult doctrine. They were simple, practical people trying to describe the uniqueness they had experienced in Jesus, and the impression he had made on them. As Adam Bede said, "Doctrine is like finding names for your feelings." Culture and language having changed, some of the New Testament metaphors listed, and others not listed, like 'Prophet', 'Priest' and 'King' are not now as helpful for communicating what we believe about Jesus as they once were. Many today think of a prophet as one who has 'second sight' rather than in the Biblical sense of a spokesman for God. They think of a priest, not as one who bridges the gap between humanity and divinity, but as one who officiates at Mass. To many in our modern world the concept of kingship is no longer acceptable.

One metaphor which has remained unaffected is John's magnificent description of Jesus as the Word of God. It still conveys with clarity why the incarnation had to be and what it meant for mankind at the time and ever after. Just as our words are the expression of our thoughts and personalities, revealing them to others, so the Word of God is the expression of God's mind and innermost nature.

It is sometimes not easy to fathom what is actually going on in the mind of another or to penetrate their inmost thoughts, likes and dislikes. We may hazard a guess but we will never know for certain unless those concerned are willing to reveal them to us. For such communication words are the prime medium. John tells us how in the life of Jesus, in the robes not of a conqueror or king but of a carpenter, God revealed the kind of God he is and how he thinks about us and is disposed towards us. In that solitary life God spelled out his inmost thoughts and nature in human terms, the only terms we can really understand. "The word was made flesh and dwelt among us, and we beheld his glory, the glory as of the only begotten of the Father, *full of grace and truth.*'' What good news this was! They now knew that caring love was at the heart of the universe, for in Jesus they had seen such love befriending outcasts and strangers, forever going the second and all the other miles.

The best we know of man and the best we know of God are revealed in Jesus. The more man allows himself to become a channel of divine love in the world, the more human he becomes. From first page to last the Bible teaches that the true dwelling place of God is the heart of man, that God longs to dwell not in the remote corners of the heavens, but in the minds and souls of his people, empowering them to love and serve. God longs that we might all become more like Jesus who was so God-conscious, whose life so vibrated to the divine life, that his hands were able to heal the sick, that he made the power and wisdom of God a reality to others.

Jesus is what God means by man. He is also what man means by God. We say, 'Like father, like son.' With Jesus the saying may be reversed, 'Like Son, like Father.' We must think of God in the light of Jesus Christ. This has to be stressed, for many heresies have arisen and still arise from keeping the character of God and the character of Jesus in separate watertight compartments and failing to equate them. Calvin depicted God as one who, in the words of Robert Burns,

> Sends ane to heaven and ten to hell
> A' for *Thy* glory
> And no for ony gude or ill
> They've done before Thee

Karl Barth rightly accused Calvin of separating his thinking about divine providence from Jesus Christ. Few could imagine Jesus sending people to Hell *just for His glory.* ''I like Jesus but I do not like God,'' said a little girl. The mother of a lad who was killed on active service shortly before the cease-fire said, ''Isn't it like God to do a thing like that?'' It is very doubtful if that same mother could have brought herself to say, 'Isn't it like Jesus to do a thing like that?'' Some mistakenly attribute many things to the will of God, and call certain happenings 'acts of God' which are completely out of character with Christ.

There has never been a time in Christian history when the mind of the Church has been more imperfectly satisfied with its interpretation of the central fact of Jesus and his relationship to God. "You can no more imprison the living, loving Risen Christ in a form of words than you can capture a perfume in a net," said James Denney. The creeds were glorious attempts to express what the Church must always try to express, but never can fully express. Celebrating as they do the greatest of all mysteries, God become man, they are more properly sung than spoken.

Though there are many aspects of the Godhead which our finite minds will never fully understand, for we "see through a glass darkly", yet fundamental to Christianity is the belief that nothing can be true of God which contradicts what has been revealed in God's human face, in Jesus Christ. This we do see and know! As Archbishop Ramsay said, "In the Father there is no unChrist-likeness at all."

In calling Jesus divine we are really making a statement more about God than about Jesus. Belief in the divinity of Jesus is essentially belief in the 'Jesus-likeness' of God. Jesus is the starting point for learning who God is. In thought and feeling, outlook and compassion, character and purpose, God is like Jesus. In coming to know the mind of Christ, we come to know the mind of God.

DOUBTS ABOUT THE RESURRECTION

Professor C.E.M. Joad said that if he were given the opportunity of interviewing one famous person of the past, he would choose Jesus of Nazareth and he would ask him what he believed was the most important question in the world: "Did you or did you not rise from the dead?"

The Bible is clear and emphatic in its answer. "On the third day he rose from the dead." Christianity broke on the world as the religion of the resurrection. The disciples who fled into hiding after the crucifixion did not reappear in the streets of Jerusalem preaching the fatherhood of God and the brotherhood of man. It was the resurrection they proclaimed. It throbs through almost every word the early Christians spoke. There is scarcely a sermon in the Book of Acts which does not state the Church's belief in the resurrection. The ethical and social implications of what Christ said followed later. In the New Testament everything hinges on the resurrection.

If it were not for the resurrection, the story of the life and teaching of Jesus, moving and sublime though they were, would probably have been buried with him in a stone-sealed tomb. It is doubtful if one word of the New Testament would have been written. The resurrection is not a belief that grew up within the Church. It is the very keystone of the Church's faith, the belief around which the Church itself grew up. Had a newspaper article been written about Kim Philby, the British Secret Service Agent, before it was known that he was a counter-spy working for Russian Intelligence, the article would probably have taken the form of an appreciation of his services to Queen and Country. In the light of the later discovery of his communist affiliations, his whole career had to be reconsidered. Everything he had said and done was now seen in a different light. Even his wife had to reassess her marriage. "Why did he marry me? How sincere was he? Was he simply using me as one more pawn in the game of betraying Britain?"

Though Philby bears no resemblance to Jesus, the analogy, I believe, is helpful for it was in the light of what finally happened to Jesus, his death and resurrection, that the early Christians re-interpreted what he had said and done. They now knew who it was that had been in their midst for three years. The resurrection was not just one more fact to add to others already known about Jesus. It threw new light on everything that had gone before. To excise the resurrection from the New Testament and from the story of the Christian Church would be like taking the hub from a wheel, the hub into which all the spokes fit. Peter, Stephen, Paul, Polycarp of Smyrna, Livingstone of Africa, Kagawa of Japan, Mother Teresa of Calcutta, Martin Luther King of America, all testify with one voice, "Christ is alive. He has had dealings with us and we with him."

How did Jesus' followers who had seen him being put to death come to be convinced that he was still alive? The gospel writers give two answers. One is the empty tomb, the other his appearances to a goodly number of his followers. The gospels record the fact that on the Sunday morning the tomb in which Jesus' body had been laid was found to be empty. At first this discovery only brought greater perplexity. The women who went early to anoint his body were not anticipating the resurrection. The transforming moment which occurred when they suddenly realised what had happened is described by Mark and Matthew in terms of an angel assuring them, "He is not here. He has been raised." In Luke's account "two men in shining garments" make a similar announcement. It should incidentally be noted that whenever the Biblical writers, who fortunately were not cursed with our literal minds, speak of "angels" or "messengers in shining garments", it is by way of affirming God's presence and power in the events that have taken place, and by way of intimating that insight into their deeper significance is being revealed.

The earliest known recital of the facts of the resurrection occur in the 15th chapter of Paul's first letter to the Corinthians which was written before any of the gospels. Speaking of "things most surely believed", Paul says,

> Christ died... He was buried... He was raised on the third day...
> He appeared to Cephas, then to the twelve. Then he appeared to
> more than five hundred brethren at once, most of whom are still
> alive. Then he appeared to James, then to all the apostles. (1 Cor.
> 15:3-7)

Paul seems to be saying, "If anyone doubts what I am saying about the resurrection of Jesus, he is free to interrogate those mentioned." Peter and James were still alive. So were most of the apostles and those five hundred brethren.

The reference is to a particular series of resurrection appearances, unique in character and confined to a limited period. In the gospels these incidents are reported in various stories, some stating the bare minimum of fact, some told at greater length with deliberate artistry. But the essential pattern is the same. The disciples are 'orphaned'. Then suddenly Jesus is with them again. At first there is amazement, with a few, doubt and hesitation, but then with overwhelming certainty they recognise who he is.

Those who experienced the mystery of the resurrection knew that they were confronted with a reality which exceeded the capacities of their eyes, ears, reason and imagination. The Risen Christ appeared in a different bodily form, bearing the marks of crucifixion, yet now strangely independent of certain earthly limitations. In Mark's Gospel we read, "After that he appeared in another form to two of them...." The Greek word for 'form' is 'morphe', the root of our word metamorphosis. We speak of a caterpillar metamorphosing into a quite different form, that of a butterfly. Some believe it was a similar process through which Jesus passed, because the New Testament evidence suggests some continuity between his pre- and post-resurrection forms, but also marked differences. This would certainly help to explain why the disciples did not at first recognise him. But it is surely wiser to admit frankly that the exact nature of our Lord's resurrection body is a great mystery.

The difficulty which confronts those who refuse to believe the resurrection is how to explain the radical change in the disciples. After Jesus' arrest, hopelessness and despair gripped the disciples. They had surrendered everything to follow Jesus. All they hoped for centred on him. But now he was dead. Terrified that the Jewish leaders might arrest them next, they crept into an upper room like frightened animals. The Jesus-movement seemed about to fizzle out like a damp squib as the Order of the Round Table did after King Arthur's death. Yet suddenly, a few days later, these same disciples became the nucleus of the greatest reforming movement this world has known. Something obviously happened to cause the Church to rise from this inferno of grim despair. And I just don't believe it happened simply in their minds. These men were not going to be convinced by anything other than solid, substantial reasons that Jesus had risen from the dead. Because personal reasons for faith in the Risen Christ are often dismissed as purely subjective, let me list some of the psychological and historical reasons why I believe in the resurrection.

I cannot otherwise account for the gathering together of the disciples to form the nucleus of the Christian Church. "The birth and rapid rise of the Christian Church remain an unsolved enigma for any historian who refuses to take seriously the only explanation offered by the Church itself." (C.F.D. Moule)

I cannot otherwise account for the change in Peter. On the night of Jesus' arrest, his concern was to dissociate himself from Jesus with whom it was dangerous to be friendly. Yet a few days later this same Peter, far from trying to save his own skin, far from denying all connection with Jesus, refuses to stop preaching about Jesus and the God who raised him from the dead.

I cannot otherwise explain why the early Church set in the forefront of their creed the affirmation about "God the Father Almighty". We would not have deduced that from the crucifixion.

I cannot otherwise account for the inclusion of the women's testimony to the empty tomb. Had such evidence been fabricated, men rather than women would obviously have been portrayed as making the initial discovery, because the testimony of a woman was invalid in law at that time.

I cannot otherwise account for the disciples acting as though death was no longer of any account. For centuries tyrants have known that the most powerful force they can use to manipulate people is their love of life and fear of death. But it did not work with the Christians. They were not afraid to die.

I cannot otherwise account for the fact that after the resurrection the disciples, all of them Jews, convinced believers in one God, not only boldly claimed that Jesus was Lord over all things in heaven and earth, but refused to rest until the whole earth acknowledged him as its rightful Lord. A Jew from Nazareth–Lord of all Creation! Proud Caesar, master of the Roman Empire, must now bow down and acknowledge himself to be the subject of this Galilean! How absurd it must have sounded. Yet three centuries later the Roman Emperor Constantine did just that, acknowledging that he and his empire could find their true life only as subjects of Jesus Christ, the King of kings.

I cannot otherwise account for the disciples, who had worshipped with Jesus in the synagogue most Sabbaths, assembling for worship, not on the Sabbath, the Saturday, but on the following day. This they called the Lord's day, the day on which they celebrated the resurrection. Institutions sanctified by the law of God and hallowed by centuries of observance are not easily or lightly changed. Imagine the consternation if it was suggested that worship services in Scotland would in future be held on a Saturday or Monday, and not on the Sunday!

Unless we are going to stop seeking causes for events, we must allow that something extraordinary happened that first Easter. It is significant that the early Christians compared the resurrection to what they regarded as the two greatest acts of God in history, the creation of the world and the exodus from Egypt. The resurrection was much more than a dramatic escape from a sealed grave. It was more than the reanimation of one who had died. It was seen by the Early Church as proof of the integrity of the universe, God's seal of approval on Jesus, God vindicating the dreams for which Jesus had lived and died, God's powerful reminder that suffering and apparent failure do not have the last word in his world. The resurrection was the culminating episode in the life of one who loved as no-one ever loved, one who did God's will as no one else ever quite did it, one who was unique in character, person and work.

Dr Archie Craig once told how the birds in his back garden show a sensitive awareness of the world about them. But as Dr Craig also pointed out, they would be mistaken if they supposed that the newspapers he read were meaningless because unintelligible to them, or if they supposed that he had not in fact reversed his car out of his garage because that is a feat they are unable to perform. Being humble creatures the birds entertain no such notions, but are learning more and more to trust Dr Craig who feeds them. Likewise to say, as some people do, that God could not possibly have raised Jesus from the dead is to make greater claims for our present knowledge and for the human intellect than we have a right to make. Is man's mind really the measure of all things? What we deem impossible may be elementary to the God who created this infinitely complex and wonderful universe. Being humble folk, the members of the Early Church said quite simply, "This is the Lord's doing and it is marvellous in our eyes."

CHAPTER SEVEN
DOUBTS ABOUT FAITH

Christianity is pre-eminently the religion of faith. Whereas the word faith occurs only twice in the Old Testament, it occurs over two hundred times in the New Testament which is only a fraction of the size of the Old. If we widen the faith category to include related words like 'believe', the New Testament figure rises markedly but the Old Testament figure only slightly.

In the ancient world wisdom, justice, temperance and courage were regarded as the four fundamental virtues. The early Christians added three more—faith, hope and love. "The greatest of these," said Paul, "is love." In our day the most neglected and misunderstood is faith.

Part of the problem is that both in the Bible and in common usage the word faith has several distinct meanings. When we speak of the Westminster Confession of Faith, the word refers to a collection of beliefs, propositions, or 'right doctrines' to which many of our Scottish forebears gave uncritical mental assent. When on the other hand we speak of having faith in someone or something, we mean that we have confidence in that person or thing. To have faith in a friend or a doctor means that you trust him to the full. To have faith in a surveyor means that you will put in an offer for a house on the basis of his report. To have faith in a compass involves being willing to trust the compass even though you think that north lies in another direction.

In other everyday phrases like 'keeping faith' or 'breaking faith with someone' the element of loyalty figures prominently. In the words 'Keep the faith, baby!' faith stands for more than intellectual belief. It stands for those convictions which are basic to a person's thinking and way of life, and which he hopes will govern the lives of those he loves. To keep the faith we must have some understanding of what we believe. There must also be a willingness to act on the basis of our beliefs. But often in the history of the Church and in the lives of individual Christians these two essential aspects of Christian faith, content and commitment, theology and trust, have been divorced.

George Eliot says of one of the characters in Adam Bede, "Hatty was one of those people who have god-fathers and god-mothers, who know their catechism, have been confirmed and have gone to church every Sunday, and yet for any practical result of strength in life or trust in death, have never appropriated a single Christian idea." We all know real life Hatties, people who guard the beliefs they inherit from their parents as they would a set of precious jewels. Though they seldom live on the basis of them, they would strongly protest if a son or daughter were to question their genuineness. It is perfectly possible to believe the Bible from cover to cover, to accept all that the Church teaches, to be glib and wordy about spiritual matters, and yet to lack most of the distinguishing marks of genuine Christian faith. Torquemada the Cardinal Inquisitor was baptised, ordained and elevated to the high office of Cardinal. He believed all that the creeds said, and yet seldom in history has anyone been more divorced from the spirit of Christ.

Martin Luther, who in the 16th century brought the word 'faith' back into prominence in the Church, stressed that it is not sufficient that we believe what the creeds say about God. "Such faith is more a form of knowledge than faith... Men possessing it can say, repeating what others have said: 'I believe there is a God. I believe that Christ was born, died, rose again for me.' But what real faith is and how powerful a thing it is, of this they know nothing..." Luther was not minimising the importance of creeds or theology. All his life he was concerned to reach a deeper understanding of the faith to which he had committed himself, and to correct the misconceptions and perversions of Christian truth which were being propounded by the church of his day. He knew that creeds and theology have an important role to play in the life of the Church. They help to clarify and define the gospel for those who will not long remain content with an irrational religion. In our theological thinking we may reach wrong conclusions, give wrong answers to right questions, or frame definitions and doctrines that are inadequate; but define and explain we must if we are to worship God with our minds and if we are to know and communicate what we believe.

The formulation and mental acceptance of certain beliefs ought never, however, to be a substitute for living the Christian life, just as hugging a timetable or guide-book is no substitute for making the journey. Faith divorced from deeds is barren. During the struggle which the church in Germany had with the Nazis in the 1930's many prominent church members who had previously made conspicuous profession of their faith became strangely silent and finally left the church. But fortunately there were others within the church, like Bonhoeffer, Niemöller, Schneider and many other unremembered 'heroes', who were prepared to protest against the inhuman doctrines of Nazism. "Not you Herr Hitler, but God is our Führer." They became valiant protestors, even though this involved risking livelihood and life. Their faith was more than an inherited treasure or an intellectually satisfying philosophy. It was the rudder by which they steered their course, not just the flag under which they sailed.

In a church in the Midwest of America, cards were placed in the pews for the benefit of visitors. Printed at the top were the words, "This church does not commit its members to any creed or profession, but there are certain truths for which we consistently stand." There then followed a list of these truths. Those who prepared the wording had unwittingly come closer to the real meaning of faith than many more orthodox Christians. Faith is determined not by those things we would like to believe, or feel we ought to believe but by those things we hold on to with conviction, those things for which we consistently stand. Our actions and dispositions shed light on what we really believe.

For faith to be Christian there must be a close connection between believing that such and such is the case and living our lives in the light of the fact that such and such is the case. 'Faith in' and 'Belief that' belong inseparably together. We could not trust ourselves to Jesus Christ if we knew nothing about him. When the theological content of faith is, however, divorced from commitment, faith is reduced to the dry intellectualism which repelled Lewis Grassic Gibbon. In *Sunset Song* he makes one of his characters say, "The Scots have never really believed. The Kirk has just been a place to collect and argue and criticise God." When on the other hand commitment is divorced from a correct understanding of God and his purposes for the world, the result is a vaguely defined Christianity that is powerless against the aggressive non-religious faiths of our day.

Jesus was concerned to indicate what believing in God should mean for daily living. It is to live without anxiety. It is to be merciful to others, for the divine governance of the world is such that 'with the judgment you pronounce and the measure you deal out will be the measure you get'. It is to 'turn the other cheek' and 'go the second mile', not returning evil for evil but being all inclusive in one's love, 'so that you may be sons of your Father who is in heaven.'

Jesus did not say as the Church has sometimes said, "Believe this creed or perish" Instead he appealed and still appeals to the instinct for truth in the human heart. He said in effect, "Search your hearts and you will see that what I have said is true." He was concerned that we should live in such a way as to fulfil the highest possibilities of our nature. The world is so constituted that to live in it in the manner Jesus described, trusting God's promises and loving our neighbours as we love ourselves, is to build life on enduring foundations. Simply to serve one's own selfish interests is to go 'against the grain of things', to court unhappiness and spiritual bankruptcy.

"By faith Abraham when he was called, obeyed." There are some things in life we cannot obey until we first believe them. The content of faith has sometimes to come before the commitment. But there are also some things we cannot believe until we first obey them. The commitment has to come first. A German engineering professor told how he never used to appreciate the music of Bach, music which enthralled countless others. At last, with what was perhaps an engineer's pragmatic gusto, he decided he would get at Bach. So he joined the famous Bach Bethlehem choir, and for a year attended all the rehearsals and sang in their concerts. At the end he said, "It was not until I sang Bach that I learned Bach from the inside." So it is with faith. We can get religion in the evangelist's tent or in the Gothic cathedral, but faith comes by responding to the truth, relevance and power that we encounter in the life and teaching of Jesus.

When Peter and Andrew first responded to Jesus' call to follow him, their faith was like a grain of mustard seed. They responded with all that they then knew of themselves to all that they knew of Jesus. Several years later Peter knew a great deal more about Christ and about himself than he did when he left his nets. That is the way of faith. There are regions of spiritual understanding that are accessible only to those prepared to love, trust and follow what in their heart of hearts they know to be true. The lives of many are impoverished because they refuse to be faithful to their best insights. My own faith is unashamedly faith in the God Jesus believed in. Though well aware that the good often suffer and the wicked often prosper, and that in any town there is grief enough to make strong men weep, yet I am prepared to trust Jesus when he spoke of the world as being in the hands of a loving God. Everything else he said was so profoundly true. As he hung on the Cross it was to this loving Father that he commended his spirit.

"Be still my soul.... in every change he faithful will remain." The calmest souls I know are those who believe this, not with the top of their minds but with the bottom of their hearts, those who are convinced that the final issues of this world lie not with the dicators or the democracies, not in disease or death, but in the hands of a heavenly Father. Martin Luther's own faith was ultimately trust in one whom he had found to be trustworthy. When threatened with death for criticising the Roman Church he replied, "Death. Death be hanged. The Lord has promised me I shall live. This I believe."

The very real temptation to take shelter in an outward orthodoxy while refusing to commit oneself, to believe *that* rather than to believe *in*, is highlighted in an address which the Rev. Percy Thomas once gave entitled 'The Tyranny of Words'. He said that when he stood for ordination he was faced with an hour-long bombardment of theological questions from people who were apparently determined that the young minister would perpetuate their orthodox theology not his own experience of the gospel. The chairman was especially keen to get him to agree to a particular theory of the atonement. But he stood his ground and finally said, "Doctor Hallock, I know that you want me to say what went on between God and Jesus when Jesus died on Calvary. I do not know and you do not know, but one thing I do know and that is that Jesus means everything to me and my spiritual life, and will be everything in my preaching if this Council decides to ordain me.'' That understandably brought silence.

To let God reproduce in our lives something of the compassion, graciousness and humility of Christ is the burning need of our time. We need not more beliefs but more belief, more commitment to Christ and what he stands for.

CHAPTER EIGHT

DOUBTS ABOUT CONVERSION

We talk a great deal today about the need for urban renewal. We speak glibly about transforming whole communities. Yet at the same time many have stopped believing in the possiblity of transforming or reforming individuals, at least once they have reached adolescence. In James Baldwin's novel *Go Tell it on the Mountain*, Elizabeth poses the question, "Don't you think the Lord can change a person's heart?" Florence replies, "I done heard it said often enough, but I got yet to see it. These niggers running around talking about that the Lord done changed their hearts... They got the same old black hearts they was born with. I reckon that the Lord done give them those hearts, and honey, the Lord don't give them no second helpings, I'm here to tell you."

Within the Church, as well as outside it, there are those like Florence who believe that 'you cannot change human nature', that 'you cannot teach an old dog new tricks', that people will continue to be what environment and heredity have made them. Such doubts about conversion strike at the heart of the Church's life for everything the Church stands for hinges on the belief that human nature can be changed by the power of God and that people can be brought to think differently and act differently. Throughout the world for almost two thousand years the Church has offered her wares; her cry has been "New lives for old!" If this offer is not valid, then most of what we do and say in the Church is little more than playing games.

Those of us who have searched long and often for a parking place in New York would be tempted to agree with the man who said of that bustling city that the only way to get a parking place is to buy a car that is already parked! But I cannot agree with those who apparently believe that the only way to become a Christian is to arrange to have yourself born into a Christian family.

Many doubts about conversion stem from the word having been degraded by unfortunate associations. To some conversion suggests emotions out of control. It carries memories of high-powered evangelistic rallies and revivals and of the sawdust trail appeal to enter a never-never land of religious delusion.

In the thinking of many the word is associated with the grosser and more disreputable sins, with the villain who becomes a hero, the prostitute who gives up her trade, the murderer who reforms his ways. Thank God such radical transformations do take place. One of the most moving contemporary evidences of this was the televised memorial service for the Rev. Tom Allan. In the congregation were many 'non-churchy' faces, hard scarred faces, yet transfigured with a strange beauty, men more acquainted with the interiors of prisons and model lodging-houses than any home, women formerly acquainted with the city's red-light areas, all gathered there to thank God for a Glasgow minister who had worked himself to death that they and others like them might find new life. But having said that, let us not forget that it was to a religious leader of enviable reputation that Jesus spoke about the need for rebirth or conversion.

Another reason for conversion being unfashionable is that since the time of Freud, psychology has laid such stress on the antecedents of human behaviour that some can scarcely believe a new start is possible. Instead of believing as Wordsworth did that we enter life trailing clouds of glory, many believe they enter life dragging chains wrought by their genes, thoughtless parents and an uncaring society, that they are merely puppets manipulated by psychological or sociological strings. Whereas the wise see life as a mix of heredity, environment and freedom, the not so wise lightly dismiss the concept of freedom and human accountability. We might paraphrase Shakespeare's famous lines and say, "The fault dear Brutus, is not in ourselves, but in our heredity and environment." Dr Barclay used to tell of a bright lad who returned home from school with a most unsatisfactory report. As his father read it, his brows furrowed. Before he could make any comment, the son inquired, "Dad do you think it is heredity or environment?" A teenage girl with a smattering of psychology said to her mother, "Do you recall that night when I wanted to talk to you about my first date, and you were too busy?" When her mother replied that she did remember, the girl added, "You destroyed me that night." This idea that we are no more responsible for our actions than a thermometer is for frost is irresponsible nonsense. It has needlessly created acute guilt complexes in the minds of many concerned parents, and caused a whole generation of young people to allow their past to tyrannise their future.

Our scepticism about conversion is further heightened because most of us prefer the orderly transmission of faith through Christian nurture. Conversions are too disruptive. We are not at home with the unpredictable.

Conversion has also been consistently misrepresented by thinking of it as an event of inner experience and private feeling that issues in purely domestic virtues and that has little or no spill-over into social, political and economic spheres. I have long been embarrassed by the kind of hot-house religiosity to which some people are converted. It can be a narrow and highly opinionated form of self-righteousness which refuses to listen to those who are not of a like mind.

But the fact that conversion has been so misrepresented and degraded does not justify our not believing in it. To dismiss the reality of conversion is to say farewell to Peter, Paul, Augustine, John Wesley, Francis of Assisi, William Grenfell and C.S. Lewis, to name but a few. These made an impact for good in their own day and on succeeding generations. When Jesus said to Peter, James and John, "Follow me", they were no worse than others, but their mental and moral state was not very high. Their love of status was the cause of those jealous quarrels for the highest places, the sound of which is heard in the gospels. In spite of his name 'Rocky', Peter was swayed like a reed, at the mercy of his hasty impulses. James and John were justifiably called "Sons of Thunder". Their request that Jesus should call down fire from heaven on the Samaritans was in keeping with their stormy natures. Initially they misunderstood their Master's aims at almost every turn. It was possibly not as hard for them to leave their nets and boats as we sometimes imagine, for they believed that in the company of Jesus many wordly rewards and honours awaited them.

Yet look at these same men a few years later. Observe the kind of life they now live. Listen to the wisdom of what they say and write. The old wordly idea of the kingdom is gone. The concern of these once fiercely nationalistic Jews is now to help God establish a kingdom characterised by justice, truth and love, a kingdom no longer for Jews alone, its gates wide open to every nation. For the sake of strangers and foreigners they are now prepared to give up home and country. The cowardice which forsook Christ and fled is gone. The longing for the chief places is now also gone.

There would be fewer doubts about conversion if the Church had stressed more that conversion does not mean being religious in a particular way. Nor does it mean cultivating some form of asceticism or using pious religious phrases. It involves becoming more fully human, more interested in others, more willing to serve like Christ in the muck and ruck of ordinary life. When over a hundred years ago the Danish philosopher Kierkegaarde tried to describe 'the whole Christian,' his contemporaries could not grasp the naturalness of the person depicted.

Some like C.S. Lewis, Monica Furlong and Zaccheus can point to a decisive turning point in their lives. Brought by force of circumstance, or some disappointment or some personal encounter to take a serious look at the 'department of the interior', many don't like what they see. Writing of his conversion C.S. Lewis said,

> For the first time I examined myself with a seriously practical purpose. And there I found what appalled me; a zoo of lusts, a bedlam of ambitions, a nursery of fears...."

Others suddenly become aware that they have forgotten or ignored God and the kingdom of the spirit. In *With Love to the Church*, Monica Furlong writes,

> When I became a Christian it happened because to begin with I had been moved by the charity and the confidence of one priest. I had never before seen anyone so relaxed, so unworried about religion, and I could see that out of the supreme certainty it gave him he could be more generous than most people to those who disagreed with him. There was no need to harangue people, to judge them or needle them. God to him was a fact of life and he proceeded to live in

acknowledgement of it; a phenomenon which moved me as few things in my life have moved me.

Many experience such moments when in their heart of hearts they know that the successful self the world sees is really a facade and that the tinselled toys they chase after have no enduring satisfaction. Jesus is a rebuke to all that is unworthy in our lives. Zaccheus found it so. What delighted Jesus was that Zaccheus was now facing in the right direction, willing to start on a pilgrimage of self-discovery and self-fulfilment as a child of God.

Rebirth, like birth, is not an end state. It is more a beginning than an arrival. Growth and widening awareness are necessary developments. We do not become saints overnight. Perhaps instead of speaking of Christians we should speak of those who are becoming Christian, whose minds are opening more and more to Christian truth, whose hearts and ears are becoming more sensitive to the suffering of humanity, who are growing in their relationships with other people and God. Gabriel Marcel wrote,

> I can in no sense boast of having arrived. I am convinced that I see more clearly than I did, though 'convinced' is a word at once too weak and too intellectual. Perhaps it would be better to say this; the freer and more detached parts of me have struggled up into the light; but there is still much of me that lies in the shadow, untouched by the almost level rays of the dawning sun; much of me that is still unevangelised.

It is significant that the early Christians were first referred to as 'followers of the way'. The maturity of our faith, said Paul, is not that we have attained, but that we 'keep striving'. John Newton said much the same, "I am not what I ought to be, I am not what I wish to be, I am not what I hope to be; but by the grace of God I am not what I was."

Maida Dugan writes in a letter to "A.D." dated November 1972

> At intervals through the years I have been prodded into self-examination by an evangelical sermon or by a personal testimony of someone who had been 'saved'. Over the years I have continued to

hope that sometime, somewhere, I would feel a burning, cleansing within my heart and soul, that I would be sure Jesus had come into my life, and that I would know I had been saved.

But this just did not happen. For years I taught a Sunday school class for young married people. A member of the class, who had graduated from a famous Bible institute, came to see me one afternoon. In the course of the visit she said, "You are a good person, Maida. You are a fine teacher, and we love you. But have you been saved.?"

"I really am not sure", I told her regretfuily... The silence that followed had to be broken by one of us, so I asked, "How can I know whether or not I am really saved?" "Oh you will know without doubt when it happens", she assured me. "Your life will be changed; you will find a great inner peace and God will be very real to you."

"Then", I sadly admitted, "I guess it has not yet happened to me." My friend asked me to kneel there in my own livingroom while she prayed that God might reveal himself to me. I was sure then and am sure today that she had experienced a real conversion. But I could not feel it, and I never have.

My husband was an elder in the church and one of my sons became a minister. I worked along my steady course as a wife, mother, teacher and friend. But often in moments of reflection I wondered why I had never had the experience of being born again.

My husband died suddenly, quietly one evening as he read the evening paper... I silently called for strength to accept this most tragic loss of my life. A deep calm came over me. I called my family members by long distance and remained strong and composed during the sad days that followed.

It was a short time after this that I finally understood why I had not found God in a born-again experience at a critical moment of my life. He had been with me always. I remembered as a child sitting in a rope swing as the first twinkling stars came into the evening sky, and asking him to help me stop my childish habit of fibbing which disturbed my parents deeply. I had gone to bed feeling secure, relieved, with a conscience clear.

At 18 I had a ruptured appendix. In those days before miracle drugs, doctors held small hope of recovery from this frightening condition. I had drifted into the blessed relief of ether, feeling it was too far back to health to make it again, willing to be taken or left as God chose, confident of his presence and care. Major surgery several times in later years was accompanied by this same peaceful feeling as I lay still and entrusted my life to God. As I review my life, I realise God has taken over many times while I waited quietly... In moments of exquisite joy, in moments of devastating grief, without my asking, he was there... He did not fight my battles for me or set up odds in my favour. But he was a part of the humility with which I accepted success, as I realised it was not my own doing. He was part of the grace with which I endured failures. Our contacts have been quiet, undramatic, natural... I no longer look for the great experience. I am sure many people have had it, and I am happy for them. But I have not.

Such an honest statement is a necessary corrective to our thinking of God primarily in terms of the unusual, blinding visions and spine-tingling experiences.

Many people are brought up to believe that the more spectacular or extraordinary an experience is, the more likely it is that God had something to do with it. They secretly worry because they have never undergone such a traumatic conversion experience. How mistaken this is. Just as a child is not aware of food and drink being changed into bone and muscle, and just as we do not feel a wound or bruise healing, so too it most often is with the operation of God in our lives. "Divine love makes no parade." To say that the Spirit of God is only present when people are emotionally excited, is a curious limitation for people to place on God. The God who does not sign his sunsets communicates for the most part unobtrusively in the quiet deep places of the mind and heart where character and personality are built and people are made strong to face life's demands.

Dr William Barclay used to say that he had never undergone what is normally thought of as a 'conversion' or 'Damascus Road' experience. Such was the Christian quality of the home in which he was brought up that he could not recall a stage when he did not have a profound admiration for Christ. From this stemmed his concern to share with others "that mind which was in Christ Jesus". and his readiness to be used to overcome a little of the inhumanity in the world.

Life for Dr Barclay was a series of little conversions, daily turnings to God for help in his struggle with self-centredness, a struggle in which he knew there is in this life no truce. He constantly fell below what he expected of himself and what he knew Christ expected of him, but like Paul he accepted God's forgiveness and pressed on. For him the very genius of the Christian faith was that we are meant to live a lifetime of fresh starts.

Just as the secret of trees budding and flowers blooming lies in our planet entering each spring into a new relationship with the sun, so too by exposing our minds and spirits week by week to God's mind and spirit, as made known in Jesus, and by living in a close relationship with others who love God, other 'fellow-becomers', the direction of our lives can be changed, fierce passions tamed, age-old prejudices driven out, dark fears overcome and the growth of divine tendencies made possible. Some of the finest and most lasting conversions have been those of people who 'felt no conviction of sin' in the narrow sense, but who through Bible study, public worship, discussion or the example of a fine Christian life were given new insights into the meaning and purpose of life. Albert Schweitzer's life was radically transformed when he came to see that every privilege entailed a responsibility, every blessing had at its heart a demand. Our lives are ultimately dyed the colour of our thoughts, imaginations and friendships.

There is a moving passage in the Book of Acts.

> The company of those who believed were of one heart and soul, and no one said that any of the things which he possessed was his own but they had everything in common. There was not a needy person among them, for as many as were possessors of lands and houses sold them and brought the proceeds of what was sold and laid it at the apostles' feet. (Acts 4:32)

This glorious attempt at communal living failed, attracting as it did too many who were desirous of getting something for nothing. What is noteworthy however is the remarkable phenomenon behind the experiment. The possessive instinct, the 'Big I' in these early Christians had diminished to such an extent that self-centred people became self-sacrificing, their dominant thought now the good of all.

They were new people, humble stewards of the good things of life, administering them no longer selfishly but for the glory of God and the good of others. God and not the inflated ego was now the pivot round which their lives revolved. More and more they asked, not "What do I want to do?" but "What does God want me to do?" They were well on the road to becoming Christians. There was the sound of love about their lives.

Leslie Weatherhead once told of a father and son who were out walking on the beach. A bright rainbow lit up the rocks near where they walked. The boy told his father that he was going to stand in the light of the rainbow. Off he ran. To the boy the rainbow was, however, always that little bit further on. But from where his father stood, the rainbow's splendour transfigured his son. So it is with those who are on the road to becoming Christians. They often wonder whether they are making any progress. They keep falling below, not only what God expects of them, but what they expect of themselves. The goal seems to keep receding. Yet though our awareness of the still-to-be-redeemed areas in our life will increase rather than decrease, if we keep facing and walking in the right direction, and keep hungering and thirsting after righteousness, others may well see in us what we cannot see in ourselves, something of the splendour of those who step off the path of self-seeking and allow themselves to be caught up into the life and purpose of God.

CHAPTER NINE

DOUBTS ABOUT THE LOVE OF GOD

On a cold November Sunday evening in 1980, in the small hillside town of Sant' Angelo dei Lombardi, whole families were clustered round their television sets watching Juventus play Inter-Milan. Several priests were officiating at Mass in the local chapel. The atmosphere in the packed men's club having grown too smoky for Mario Corado, he slipped out for a breath of fresh air. That saved his life, for suddenly the ground beneath him exploded. Eighty per cent of the buildings in the village including all the churches were flattened within ninety seconds.

When Corado found he was still alive he picked himself up. Turning towards the bar which he owned, he saw a great pile of rubble burying his two sons and more than twenty other young people. There was not even a priest to pray for them or with him. The town's priests had been killed. "I have always been a Catholic," Corado said, "but today I cursed the Lord for what he had done. I took off my cross and threw it away."

I once watched a minister, whose salary was assured, and who was in good health, smile sweetly and tell his television audience that "God is love." In the background an electronic organ played 'gospel' music. I could forgive Corado, and I am sure God would too, if on hearing that, he had cried out, "The hell he is."

Nowhere in all literature has human tragedy been depicted with deeper insight or greater power than in the book of Job. His cattle were stolen and his servants killed. Next the wind blew down his house where his children were playing, killing them all. Shortly afterwards he was stricken with a serious illness. Though he did not accept his wife's advice to curse God, at times he came close to it. He asked some unpleasant questions. If God is all he is cracked up to be, how does it happen that houses blow down on innocent children? Why does injustice go unpunished while calamity falls on the righteous? Today people ask the same questions. Why does a fine young man die of cancer while old incontinent people who cannot remember their names linger on? Why are there so many crooks living in luxury while so many children go to bed hungry and cold? Such angry questioning of the ways of God is not blasphemy, nor presumption. It is an indication that the questioner cares and that he is concerned about justice.

What, if anything, is behind the mystery of life? Is there a friendly Presence, or is there nothing but cosmic energy and blind chance? Jean Paul Richter concluded that the throne of life is empty. In his poetic dream (or nightmare), Jean Paul Richter says, "I have traversed the world. I have risen to the suns. I have passed athwart the great waste places of the sky. There is no God. I have gazed into the gulf beyond and cried, 'Where art Thou?' And no answer came. We are orphans, you and I." Others like Mark Twain have concluded that behind the universe is a powerful but unfeeling Creator. "God does not know we are here and would not care if he did." Aristotle spoke of the Unmoved Mover. A few believe that we are at the mercy of ruthless fate or a ruthless God. Towards the end of *Tess of the D'Urbervilles*, Thomas Hardy says, "...the President of the Immortals...had ended his sport with Tess."

There are two opposing mysteries in the world, the mystery of order and goodness, and the mystery of disorder and suffering. If we believe there is a President of the Immortals who takes pleasure in inflicting pain, then the existence of so much order, beauty and sacrificial love is a great mystery. If on the other hand we affirm that there is a loving God, then the existence of disorder, disease and cruelty is a great mystery.

If random chance, operating within the blind laws of statistical probability brought the world and ourselves into being, then obviously the blind mechanism of chance is indifferent to whether we rejoice or suffer. Though in theory there should be no problem of undeserved suffering for thorough-going atheists, in practice the problem and anguish are very real. The conviction that evil and suffering are departures from what ought to be is deep-rooted. The atheist is also faced with the problem of explaining the vast amount of order and purposefulness in a world that came into being simply as a result of chance.

The Jews were more sensitive to the problem of undeserved suffering than any other nation in the ancient world for the simple reason that no other people had such faith in a just and righteous God. The Jew's confidence in the justice of God drove him to ask why good people should suffer plague, violence, cruelty and slaughter. A lady pained by great tragedy in her own life said half in jest to a Jewish friend, "If I ever make it to heaven, I'm going to line up at the throne of God and ask, 'Why did you arrange it so that things like this could happen?'" "Hattie," her friend replied, "It will be a very long line."

The poet who wrote the Book of Job wrote it because his contemporaries were settling for too easy answers to the question of suffering. Job's four friends were well-intentioned. But unfortunately they spoke too soon, said too much and said the wrong things. They have their modern counterparts. *Whose Life Is It Anyway?* is a powerful play about a man paralysed from the neck down. Never again will he get out of bed. I wish every doctor, social worker and hospital chaplain could see this play. The patient chooses to think, but the representatives of these professions prefer their platitudes; and each profession has its own. The chaplain for example tells the bed-ridden man that he must now regard himself as a vessel into which other people can pour their compassion! Throughout the play the patient probes and questions these hollow platitudinous half-truths. When he refuses to accept their pretty theories and their slick easy answers, then like Job's friends centuries before, they get very angry with him.

Some of Job's friends said that all suffering is a result of sin, and that God, being just, makes bad things happen to bad people. Job must therefore at some time in the past have committed some grave misdemeanours, even though they now escaped his memory. This inadequate explanation of suffering still lingered on in the time of Jesus. When he was asked, "Rabbi, who sinned, this man or his parents, that he was born blind?" he replied in effect, "That is far too glib and simple a question. God is not like that. He cares for bad people as well as good people. The sun and the rain, light and darkness, earthquakes and hurricanes, cancer and coronaries, fall on the just and unjust alike. Those eighteen people upon whom the tower of Siloam fell, were they more guilty than all the others living in Jerusalem? I tell you no." Those in our day who have glimpsed the bony frames of starving Ugandans, or like Mario Corado have seen some terrible disaster, find it impossible to accept the theory that all suffering is a punishment for sin.

Another explanation put forward by Job's friends was that God sends suffering to help us grow in character. Now few would deny that profound lessons can be learned from adversity, that qualities like courage, patience and compassion are often born of suffering. Most of us can think of people whose sympathies were enlarged and their insight deepened because they faced personal tragedy in the right spirit. Writing with hindsight the Psalmist said, "It is good for me that I was afflicted."

To say, however, that God allows suffering in his world and that he can use suffering to enrich life, are very different things from saying that God deliberately sends pain or adversity. To talk of cancer as being a blessing in disguise, or to say that the smoke and dust clouds which gathered over Auschwitz and Sant'Angelo dei Lombardi, were, in the words of Cowper's hymn, "big with mercy", comes as near to blasphemy as anything I know. The God revealed in the life of Jesus is not that kind of God. Jesus refused to accept evil as good. He knew that the suffering in the world is far in excess of what can be understood as a means to a good end. Throughout his ministry he waged war on disease and man's inhumanity to man. Far from willing the deaths of little children he raised Jairus' daughter from the dead. His fight against evil sometimes took the form of healing what was broken and opposing what was inhuman. At other times he simply endured the hate, the suffering and even death itself in the faith that the last word is never with these things, but with the loving purposes of God.

The facile argument that suffering helps us grow in character could logically lead to certain unattractive conclusions. "Don't attempt to rehouse those who live in slum conditions. Youngsters will have more character if they grow up in tough conditions." "Don't replace that arthritic hip. The pain will help mature the person." When Sir James Young Simpson discovered chloroform, such arguments were unfortunately used to forbid its use in childbirth.

Some point out that human beings with their inborn love of risk and adventure would not be happy in a completely safe world, a world without hazards and hardships. Others argue that it is our shortness of vision that creates the problem, that if only we were able to take the long-range view, to see suffering in the perspective of eternity rather than time, of centuries rather than weeks, then what looks bad to us just now would appear to be good! They point out how our earth would be a much less attractive place to live, had it not been for earlier massive earthquakes and volcanic eruptions which brought into being such scenic attractions as mountains and lakes.

An American friend tells how in the Kaibab Forest on the north rim of the Grand Canyon some misguided conservationists decided to befriend the deer. With the best intentions they killed off the panthers. Freed from their natural enemy the deer multiplied rapidly. After a short time they had eaten all the low browse. Then they ate the high browse. Then they nibbled away at the moss and the bark. After that there was nothing left to eat; so they starved. The lovely animals that had been saved from the panthers became food for the buzzards. The moral of the story, my friend said, is that, taking a long-range view, a panther is a deer's best friend!

There is considerable truth in all these arguments, but they would not, I am sure, bring much comfort to a deer which was being stalked by a panther, or the Italian earthquake victims, or the wife of a mountaineer who had just been killed. They might partly answer the question, but not the questioner.

Another argument in which there is considerable but limited truth is that in order to remove all 'moral evil', evil for which man is entirely responsible, God would have to reduce us to the status of puppets. Jerked by divine strings we would then unhesitatingly carry out his wishes. But in giving people 'free will' God had to take the risk that we might choose not to cooperate with him, that we might abuse our freedom and run off into far countries of rebellion. Dictators may bulldoze people and thus quickly achieve their little ends, but God, being a loving Father, has to wait, biting his lips, gripping his hands behind his back, respecting our freedom of choice even when we make the wrong choice, longing for the day when of our own free will we will return from the far country and be the kind of people he wants us to be. God refuses to make people good against their wishes, even though such restraint is often mistaken for divine indifference. "Why," cried Thomas Carlyle, "does God sit in heaven and do nothing?" But where would God stop were he to step in and remove the selfishness and evil from the world? He would surely not stop with I.R.A. bombers, nor with the violent criminals and heroin pushers. What about our greed, our cruel words and inhumanity? As the Psalmist said, "If thou, O Lord, shouldst mark iniquities, Lord, who could stand?"

Once again one has to admit that the parents of a young soldier killed in action, or of a young girl raped by a sex maniac, would not derive much comfort from this insight. There is a limit to the value of 'explanations'. Suppose God had explained to Job the mystery of his suffering. Suppose he had said that the reason the cattle were stolen, the crops ruined and his children killed was such and such, spelling out everything right down to and including the case of his boils. Job would then have had his intellectual explanation, and then what? Understanding why his children had to die, Job would still have had to face their empty chairs every morning. Carrying in his pocket a theological or medical explanation of his leprosy, he would still have had the discomfort and the pain.

In Steinbeck's book *The Grapes of Wrath*, Casey had formerly been a minister. But when we meet him in the book he has left the ministry. Why? Because preachers are, he said, supposed to know all the answers to life's baffling questions, and he could no longer provide many of them. I wonder where he got that idea of the ministry. No minister can satisfactorily answer the question as to why in a world made by a loving God there is so much suffering and heartbreak, but he can help people cope with adversity by preaching and pastoral care.

Both Paul and Job suffered greatly. Their responses to suffering were however radically different, mainly, I believe, because they had such different mental pictures of God. Job pictured God sitting serene and untouched, just watching people suffer. To Job this was the scandal and the perplexity. Paul had a radically different picture of God. He was certain that the suffering love which had been seen in the life and death of Jesus was none other than the love of God.

Dr Leslie Weatherhead tells how one night while sailing in the Mediterranean, he passed close to Stromboli, the island volcano. It was after dinner and it was dark. Suddenly from the volcanic crater huge tongues of flame shot up, lighting up the ocean for miles around. For a few hours the passengers glimpsed those great fires which had been burning at the heart of the mountain since the earth was created. Paul likewise believed that for a few years there had been seen in the life and death of Jesus the incredible suffering love which is at the heart of this universe. He viewed the Cross not as an isolated event, but as something always true about God, "just as if the log of time had been sawn through on Good Friday, revealing the rings of the grain that go right through the wood from top to bottom." (R.C.Walls)

It is doubtful whether in the history of human thought anything is more extraordinary than this, that the brutal crucifixion of Jesus, the finest person this world has known, should have caused the early Christians to marvel not just at his suffering love, but also at the suffering love of God. In his own experience Paul had also found it to be true that God, far from standing aloof from the pain of the world, suffers with us in our suffering. God had not only helped him cope with adversity but had enabled him often to turn to good what others had meant for evil. "In everything God works for good with those who love him." "In him who strengthens me I am ready for anything." Paul's faith that "God was in Christ" and that the final word is not with suffering, evil or death, changed Paul's thinking about suffering.

I reckon that the sufferings we now endure bear no comparison with the splendour, as yet unrevealed, which is in store for us... What can separate us from the love of Christ? Can affliction or hardship? Can persecution, hunger, nakedness, peril or the sword? "We are being done to death for thy sake all day long," as Scripture says; "we have been treated like sheep for the slaughter"—and yet, in spite of all, overwhelming victory is ours through him who loved us. For I am convinced that there is nothing in death or life, in the realm of spirits or superhuman powers, in the world as it is or the world as it shall be, in the forces of the universe, in heights or depths—nothing in all creation that can separate us from the love of God in Christ Jesus our Lord. (Rom. 8:18, 35ff., N.E.B.)

In Voltaire's *Candide,* Professor Pangloss suffers one misfortune after another, but nothing shakes his glib optimism. Whenever tragedy strikes he says, "All is for the best in this the best of all possible worlds." That is not the Christian view. Just because this is not the best of all possible worlds, just because it is still a world in the making, God wants us to wage war with him on poverty, famine, loneliness, greed and disease, to change the processes which produce evil and disorder into processes which produce good. He also wants us to do what we can to minimise the effects of natural disasters.

In the New Testament we find all the miseries quoted by those who deny God's love. Christianity was cradled in pain and adversity. The apostle John lived through the titanic struggle of the infant Church against the mailed fist of the Roman Empire. He had seen people of all ages tortured, burned and mauled in the arena for the sake of Christ. Yet it was he who as an old man wrote, "God is love." Christian faith in a loving father was not dreamed up in some idyllic setting remote from life's forbidding facts. Those who first carried the good news about God to the far corners of the world lived in no ivory towers. They were no strangers to adversity. There was much they did not understand, much that perplexed them, but of one thing they were absolutely certain; that behind creation there was one whom they could call Father, a Christ-like God who shares the pain of the world.

CHAPTER TEN
DOUBTS ABOUT PRAYER

"Seek ye the Lord while he may be found. Call ye upon him while he is near." (Isa. 55.6) It may come as a surprise to many to learn that these familiar words from Isaiah have nothing to do with meeting God in some quiet retreat. The prophet was saying that in the coming of Cyrus to conquer Babylon and set the Jewish exiles free, God was near. The time for active response was now. God, he said, is to be found in the events of life around us which present us with opportunities which can be missed if we do not seize them at once. The well-known text does not mean that God is 'near' in a mystical sense, but rather that he is near in the challenges of everyday life and duty. This is a much-needed reminder. Meeting with God is not confined to the religious bit of life. He is to be encountered in the whole range of contemporary life where he is active. "We must hear the voice of God in the voice of the times." said the bishops of Vatican II.

A.E. Whitman told of a prostitute he knew who met God at night in Leicester Square "in the face of a child, a child with golden curls and eyes blue as cornflowers. The sight turned her vile life to ashes in a moment." Others have been confronted by God in the haunting stare of a starving child, in the patient, forgiving love of a husband or wife, in the fidelity of a friend, in the biography of one whose life was devoted to a great cause, in a modern novel where the emptiness and futility of blind ambition is clearly revealed.

God meets us at the place of his choosing. It is, however, the verdict of men and women down the ages, that the quiet place of prayer is one of the places where we are most likely to meet him. It is therefore a matter of concern that many professing Christians, though continuing to play an active role in the Church, live with countless misgivings about prayer. They pray, if at all, with far less conviction than their parents did.

69

They wonder whether prayer is anything more than positive thinking, whether anything happens as a result of prayer which would not have happened without it. When life fails to take on the shape it would take if God were the kind of God they wanted, some stop praying. Others point to good works, generous philanthropy, social reforms, or selfless devotion to scientific research and insist that these are the devotional exercises of modern Christians. Then there are others like Victor in W.H. Auden's ballad. For Victor who has been betrayed by his wife, prayer seems like talking to somebody who either is not there or does not care.

> Victor walked out into the High Street
> He walked to the edge of the town
> He came to the allotments and the rubbish heap
> And his tears came tumbling down.
> Victor looked up at the sunset
> As he stood there all alone
> Cried: "Are you in heaven Father?"
> But the sky said, "Address not known."

Many doubts about prayer stem from inheriting wrong conceptions of prayer and unwarranted expectations about what prayer can accomplish. In the minds of many there is really little difference between praying and wishing. Both are regarded as possible means of obtaining what you want. But there is in fact an immense difference between a mere wish and a true prayer, the difference being faith in a living God.

The known character of the God to whom we pray is all important. It conditions the hopes of those who pray. The God to whom Jesus prayed was a wise Father, not a doting parent who because he has more love than sense grants whatever requests his children make. Surely no thoughtful Christian could bow his head, and in the name of Jesus who had nowhere to lay his head, who stated that 'a man's life does not consist in the abundance of his possessions', ask for a pile of diamonds or a luxury limousine or a holiday in Bermuda. We totally misunderstand Christian prayer if we think of it as a signed blank cheque drawn on the Bank of Providence.

Paul tells how he prayed three times to be rid of his 'thorn in the flesh'. It was a worthy petition, the earnest desire of a man whose entire life was dedicated to God. He prayed for better health that he might better serve Christ. It puts many of our private petitions to shame. Yet his illness was not removed. It would be interesting to write the rest of Paul's biography after the fashion of our 20th century Christianity. One of my teachers, Paul Scherer, thought it might have gone as follows.

> After these things Paul began to lose interest and fell away from the Church. His thorn was obviously there to stay. Prayer did not budge it. Perhaps he could get along just as well without prayer. So he went back to his trade and made tents. Every time God or prayer or religion was mentioned, he smiled cynically and told of his unanswered prayer. Among his last words there was something about having done a great deal better had it not been for that thorn in the flesh.

According to Luke, Paul's story finished very differently. There followed the long journey back to Miletus. "I know," he said, " 'that you shall see my face no more.'.. As he finished speaking, he knelt down with them all and *prayed*." Strange for someone who had found nothing in prayer! From Tyre, many disciples accompanied Paul until he was well out of the city. They too knelt down with him on the shore. Again how strange for someone who had found nothing in prayer! The story of the later chapters of the Book of Acts is the story of Paul constantly at prayer. He came finally to Rome to be tried before the Emperor. From prison he writes, "I kneel in prayer to the Father... that out of the treasures of his glory, he may grant you strength and power through his Spirit in your inner being." But Paul, there is nothing in prayer. Remember how your thorn was not removed!

Arnold Toynbee put his finger on one of the major causes of doubts about prayer. For many generations we have been living, he said, on spiritual capital, clinging to Christian practice without possessing Christian belief, and 'practice unsupported by belief is a wasting asset.' Ultimately prayer depends on whether we believe there is a divine power at work in the world. If we believe that, we pray. If we doubt that we do not pray.

The mighty assurance which Paul had that the Mystery behind life is in some deep and eternal sense like Jesus Christ, and the desire to link ourselves with this Christ-like God so that maybe, just maybe, he can use us for his purposes, is what prayer is all about. We smile when we read of the second year student who left college because as he put it, "I had a difference of opinion with the principal about who was running the college." Yet in the context of prayer there are many who want to run the show, to impose their thoughts and ways on God, to manipulate him for their own ends. Too many prayers are of the form, "Lord I have it all planned. Just help me to bring these plans to fruition." Others attempt to bend God's will to theirs, to change God's mind. A mother hearing her son pray after this fashion, said, "Son, don't bother to give God instructions. Just report for duty." If more people prayed, "Use me", "Change me" instead of "Give me", they would reach a deeper understanding of prayer. "The highest perfection", said Teresa of Avila, the 16th century Spanish saint, "does not consist in interior joys, nor in sumblime raptures, nor in visions, but in bringing our will into such conformity with the will of God that whatever we know He desires, that also shall be our desire." Jesus the great master of prayer asked nothing for himself except daily bread, strength for the testing, and grace to reveal God to the world. In more recent times the Kikuyu Christians, experiencing martyrdom for their faith at the hands of the Mau Mau prayed, "Lord we ask not to be safe, but to be faithful."

Doubts about prayer have also been created by lack of honesty in prayer. In a well-to-do suburban church, I once joined the congregation in repeating the prayer of General Confession.

> We have offended against Thy holy laws. We have left undone those things we ought to have done, and we have done those things that we ought not to have done, and there is *no health in us*. But Thou O Lord have mercy upon us, *miserable offenders*.

From the casual manner in which the words were recited, few would have guessed that the congregation were genuinely sorry. I strongly suspected that had someone accused one of the members of being a "miserable offender" and an "unhealthy character" legal advice would have been sought concerning defamation of character.

For various reasons many doubt the worthwhileness of prayer, but there are also many who would agree with William Law when he said that "he who has learned to pray has learned the secret of a holy and happy life." Today it is fashionable to acknowledge the greatness of people like Mother Teresa, Dag Hammarskjold, Martin Luther King, Archbishop Romero and Lech Walesa, to stress the nobility of their ethical teaching, to admire their concern for the underprivileged and the oppressed, and all the time to ignore the fact that, like Jesus, they all spent a great deal of time in prayer and meditation, and encouraged others to do so. Prayer is the empowering secret of their quality lives. Prayer has changed many people who in turn have changed many things.

When Malcolm Muggeridge went with a B.B.C. film crew to Calcutta to film Mother Teresa at work among the destitute people in Calcutta, he saw before his eyes a personality in whom prayer was vital and influential. He soon realised he could not understand her unless he understood her praying. In Mother Teresa there was that which went beyond working and caring. There was an inner sensitivity to a world of truth and power higher than herself.

There are two essential aspects of life as God intended it. The Psalmist symbolises the first in terms of "green pastures" and "still waters", an oasis of calm where we are rested and refreshed for the journey ahead; the second in terms of the "paths of righteousness". Most of us recognise as a caricature of Christianity the kind of spirituality which makes prayer meetings and retreats a substitute for treading the paths of righteousness, a substitute for costly sharing and caring. Every bit as great a caricature of Christianity is a life of constant activity with little or no time for quietness or prayer or meditation. The physical dangers of overdeveloping practical strenuousness are too obvious to linger on—high blood pressure, ulcers and coronaries. If we must run we should not run all the time; if we must burn the midnight oil we should remember that lamps need refilling. Otherwise we become restless, impatient, aggressive doers, often spreading irritability and unrest all around. It is essential that we make time to develop our responsiveness to what is healing, calming and redeeming in life. A man is not defrauding his employer when he pauses to oil his tools or whet his scythe.

"Bear ye one another's burdens." That is not easy. There

will be days when Moses' hot outburst to God will echo in our hearts. "This whole people is a burden too heavy for me: I cannot carry it alone." It is one thing to set out gallantly when the flags are waving and the drums summoning to a new crusade. It is quite another to keep plodding on when the initial impetus has spent its force and the trumpets have ceased to sound. We need to pray if for no other reason than that we all need to replenish our too soon exhausted store of enthusiasm, tenderness and serenity. Too much has been made of the well-known story of William Wilberforce and the lady who asked him whether amid his multifarious duties on behalf of the slaves, he was not perhaps neglecting his own soul. The reply was, "Madam... I almost forgot I had a soul." But the lady was not wholly wrong.

It is true that fields are not ploughed by praying over them, nor oil obtained by prayer, nor accounts balanced; but it is equally true that ploughing, drilling and book-keeping can become a drudgery unless seen in a larger context. When all day we have been dealing with the close-ups of life's details, until the meaning is drained from them, it helps to stop for a few minutes and ponder the cosmic setting in which our lives are placed and our work done. For me the essential meaning of prayer is summed up in the phrase, 'Times of Awareness.' Prayer can make us more aware of God's plans for the world and his hopes for us.

If the aim of life is to fulfil the purpose for which God created us, then it is important before huffing and puffing and working up a sweat, that we make time to learn what God would have us do. Rushing about constantly seeking to control things, it is easy to lose sight of the spiritual aims for which we should be controlling them. Herodotus claimed that the bitterest sorrow is to aspire to do much and achieve nothing. Not so — the bitterest sorrow is to aspire to do much and to do it — and then to discover it was not worth doing. Action is important only if directed towards right goals. Times of quiet can be therapeutic, an antidote to the nervous anxiety which cripples so many lives. Anxieties often stem from our priorities being so unchristian. We worry about not being able to afford a certain style of life, about what other people are thinking about us, about where they are placing us on the social ladder. Prayer serves as a reminder that what others think of us is a small thing compared to what God thinks of us. Prayer can also serve as a powerful reminder of what really matters in life and what does not matter all that much.

The Bible is full of challenges to activity. 'Building', 'fighting', 'marching' are common Biblical metaphors. But equally common are words like 'waiting', 'resting', 'abiding'. "They that wait upon the Lord shall renew their strength." "In quietness and confidence shall be your strength." "Be still and know that I am God." "Come unto me all that labour and are heavy laden and I will give you rest." "Come ye yourselves apart and rest awhile." We need to make time to give the Highest a hearing. We need to get away regularly from the world with its false valuations, its mad scramble for reputation and honours, its unlovely and impure thoughts and ponder on what is lovely and of good report. "Our lives are dyed the colour of our imaginations." (Marcus Aurelius)

A woman was once in a lawyer's office. Her husband was critically ill in hospital. A will was being drawn up for him to sign. Many charitable organisations would benefit from it. "Are you sure this is what your husband wants done?" the lawyer asked. When the lady replied in the affirmative, the lawyer inquired, "How are you sure?" "Because," she replied, "we have lived together over forty years and we have been very close." That is the nearest parallel I know to the influence of prayer.

The analogy of prayer as friendship with God is a helpful one. It reminds us of certain basic things about prayer. We do not use friendship for our own ends. We do not go to a friend only in times of crisis. We enjoy the other personality for what he or she is. We regularly allow the other mind and personality to enrich ours. So it is with prayer. Again, friendship is not formal, but neither is it formless. It has its obligations and disciplines. We do not make friends by nodding our head to a person across the street once a month. Friendship grows with oft-repeated meetings. Through speech, listening and silence heart makes itself known to heart. So it is with prayer. Here for many is the nub of the prayer problem. We have mastered the technique of doing something to the world and to other people, but not of letting another world and other people do something to us. Many find it difficult to relax and be receptive to great music or art. Prisoners of our activism and much speaking, it is not surprising that we find stillness a problem. Many when they do pray are still go-getters, still trying to force their selfish will on God and the world.

In his book *The Art and Practice of Relaxation* Dr Ian Martin writes of the need to practise relaxation exercises *briefly* and *regularly*. "Set aside a brief time... Ideally make it the same time each day." That also holds for prayer. Dr Andrew Bonar tells in his diary of whole days given over to prayer, of nights spent in confession and intercession. It may be my own spiritual immaturity I am confessing when I say that such testimony leaves me dazed and very definitely on the outside of a locked door. I do, however, take comfort from Jesus' words that we shall not be heard 'for our much speaking.' Short sincere prayers spoken from the heart are I am sure as acceptable to God as lengthy ones and far more acceptable than prayers spoken by the lips only. The element of regularity is as important in devotional exercises as in physical exercises. If left at the mercy of inclination there will be no spiritual growth or physical build-up.

The first moments of the day are crucial. How the conscious recognition of God can help achieve a right orientation within which the whole day may be lived! Even simply saying to ourselves when we awake, "This is the day which the Lord has made. Let us rejoice and be glad in it" can help to get us out of the right side of the bed! Lord Baden-Powell taught his scouts to stand for a few minutes before the open window each morning and with arms slowly raised, to say with every deep breath, "Thank God".

During the day it is helpful to stop momentarily and thank God for those fleeting moments when we are surprised by joy, the joy of meeting a friend, of seeing a tree burst into bud, the joy of playing a game with a close friend, of walking hand in hand with a little child, of hearing someone say, "I love you", the joy of singing a lovely hymn or hearing a favourite piece of music, or sharing in worship that is meaningful. Making time to savour the joy of such experiences is surely part of what is meant by enjoying God forever.

There are also those moments when we instinctively cry, "God, I'm tired", "God, I don't know what to do", "God, I'm sorry." There are other moments when our hearts are moved with compassion for some poor soul whose path crosses ours. "God help him," we cry. Such honest heartfelt cries are the raw material of prayer. For a moment we 'let go, and let God'. The oftener we do this the more it becomes second nature.

Many find the greater peace and quiet of evening the best time for prayerful meditation. If we liken prayer to conversation in which we speak to God and God speaks to us, then it is important to remember that two very different things are meant by 'speak'. When God speaks there are no audible words. We sometimes say that a certain piece of music speaks to us. So it is with God. In prayer we listen with the soul far more than the ears. It can be helpful in our quiet times to read a short passage from the Bible or from some such devotional aid as *The Upper Room* or Dr William Barclay's *Daily Study Bible*, or from a notebook of our own making in which we have collected thoughts and passages which have moulded and enriched our lives. Having done this we should spend a few minutes thinking about the implications of what we have read for our own lives and the lives of others. We should note the thoughts, names and the needs God brings to mind during such quiet times. Just as placing a baby who is struggling for life into an incubator can often help the doctor care for the child, so I believe praying for others can make it easier for God to do what he longs to do. Paul was a good psychologist when he advised, "Let not the sun go down on your wrath." Anger churning in the mind churns on during sleep. The following morning is often turned sour as a result. The converse fortunately holds. Healthy thoughts work radiantly in our nature while we sleep. The subconscious becomes prayer's ally, doubling prayer's power. It is a pity that for many, hearing the late-night news has priority over turning their thoughts to God.

> Now I lay me down to sleep
> I've seen the news that would not keep
> If I should die before I wake
> At least I'll know what headlines make.

Meditation and prayer, when regularly practised, can help restore a degree of wholeness, purpose and vitality to our lives.

CHAPTER ELEVEN
DOUBTS ABOUT SIN

One would have thought that the doctrine of the universality of sin as stated by Paul, "All have sinned and come short of the glory of God" would have been one of the easiest doctrines for people in the 20th century to accept. Yet even within the Church there are those who regard the idea of sin as out-dated. In his book *Mature Mind* Harry Overstreet tries to free Jesus from the stigma of ever having harboured such an idea by alleging, in defiance of all the biblical evidence, that the idea of sin was first introduced into Christianity by St Augustine.

Paradoxically at the same time as the Church speaks less about sin than she used to, playwrights, press-men and scientists speak far more about it. Films are being made, plays performed and books written that are obsessed with the fact of human sin. Twisted human relationships, corruption in high places, atrocities, hatreds and immoralities of every kind are depicted in plays, films and novels, sometimes with skill and insight, sometimes vulgarly. When J. Robert Oppenheimer, the atomic scientist, was asked in his later years what most occupied his thoughts, he replied, "The evil of humanity". Our newspapers daily remind us of man's alienation from man and his inhumanity to man. Builders of houses and makers of cars are not for the most part theologians, yet they fit locks to house and car doors. They are under no illusion about human nature. The police, tax-inspectors, customs officers and judges exist because sin, far from being the creation of a disturbed mind, is the most realistic fact with which we have to deal.

The greatest thinkers of all ages like Plato, the Hebrew prophets, Buddha and Confucius, made human sinfulness the burden of their most serious thought. Shakespeare's finest plays deal with the tensions and problems sin produces. Early 20th century dramatists like Eugene O'Neill, Albert Camus and

Ernest Hemingway constantly struggled with its centrality in human life, with the dimensions and results of this inner wrongness, with the deep dissatisfaction that finally overtakes modern prodigals. The idea that the concept of sin is a belated hangover from an earlier unenlightened day finds no support in their writings.

In speaking of human sinfulness there is however a significant difference between such modern writers and the biblical writers. The difference is the dimension of God. For the biblical writers sin was more than envy, greed, drunkenness, vice and lust. It was more than a matter of wrong things done, or fine things left undone. Just as bodily pain, sickness, high temperatures and headaches are often not the disease itself, but only the signs and symptoms of it, so, say the biblical writers, the follies, crimes and corruptions of people are an indication that something is far wrong at the centre of life. There is no more profound commentary on the nature of sin than that found in the early chapters of Genesis. There we are told how Mr and Mrs Everyman rebelled against God and took creation into their own hands for their own purposes. They tried to take the created world away from God and make it their own. Wanting to run the show, they also tried to take their lives away from God and make them their own.

How modern the Genesis story is! "My life is my own. Nobody is going to tell me how to behave... I know what I want out of life and I'm jolly well going to get it... You have got to look out for Number One..." In speaking thus we make it abundantly clear that for us the pivotal centre of life is not God, but the 'Big I.'

> There was a little maiden once
> Who lived in days gone by
> Whose every thought and every word
> Always began with I.
> I think, I know, I wish, I say,
> I like, I want, I will
> From morn to night, from day to day,
> 'I' was her burden still.

According to the Bible sin is that attitude to life in which we feel we are the centre of the universe, so that everything revolves, or ought to revolve, round us. Few hold such a view intellectually, at least not in so many words. But in everyday life most people assume that their lives are theirs to do with as they please. "All we like sheep have gone astray. We have turned everyone *to his own way*."

Bruce Gunnerson's "Modern Creed" was a forceful reminder that there is no other subject which so fascinates people as themselves and their own standing in the world.

> I believe in my Income and Standard of Living, Maker of pleasure on earth; And in Things-I-Own and Things-I-Want-To-Get, which are conceived by desire for possessions, born of a regular pay-check, suffered under monthly payments, then glorified, cherished and admired. They descend in their value, but on a future day I'll acquire some more, ascending in my status, 'til I sit in quite comfortable retirement, for whence I shall come to enjoy them all without end. I believe in my home, my comfortable car, my holidays with pay, my insurance for life, the satisfaction of my wants, and a bank account ever increasing.

Old-time theologians called this arrogant self-centredness which drives people to inist on getting their own way regardless of God and everyone else, 'original sin'. Today we prefer politer psychological and sociological terms. What we call this curse that wrecks human hopes and lives is secondary. What matters is that we recognise its reality, for here we have the root cause of the follies and vices of mankind, the quarrels and the divorces, the power struggles and brutalities.

Macbeth's selfish ambitions were influenced by a strange encounter with three witches. They greeted him first as 'Thane of Glamis', then as 'Thane of Cawdor' and finally with the words, "All hail Macbeth, you shall be king hereafter." In dramatic form at the beginning of his play Shakespeare seeks to bring into the open the secret, half-suppressed desires for self-advancement and self-glorification which had been lurking in Macbeth's mind. The witches propose a goal for Macbeth's life very different from that of glorifying God or enriching his world. The tragedy that follows stems from Macbeth's succumbing to the temptation to be the 'most important one'.

The temptation is strong to look at life in terms of our own status and interests. Other people look at life in terms of theirs. I like to have more pay than others, to 'lord it over' them. Others like to have more pay than me, to lord it over me. We inevitably clash. The same is true of nations. At the root of most modern problems is the fundamental atheism with which the vast majority of people regard life and the world. Start with the assumption that the world is ours to exploit, that we are answerable to ourselves and nobody else, and nothing will come out right. It is like starting a problem in arithmetic with the assumption that two and two make five.

As a young man, the British philosopher C.E.M. Joad was a militant agnostic and vigorous critic of religious beliefs. Many were therefore surprised, after the Second World War, when he was confirmed into the Church of England. He explained that what had attracted him finally was the Christian understanding of sin, which he found made more sense than any other interpretation of the sickness of humanity.

When Archbishop Temple was a don at Cambridge, he attended an evangelistic meeting conducted by Dr Reuben Torry. He wanted to see what such a meeting would be like. Later he said to a friend, "Torry told us that in the dark of the night his sins marched past him in scarlet procession. I never feel that way. My sins are all grey." Sin can sometimes express itself in gross and terrible ways, but for most people sin cloaks itself in more respectable forms. Tyranny for example is not always of the Nazi or hammer and sickle variety. How cunningly we all try to manipulate people to our own advantage. Tyranny sometimes appears in the guise of sweetness and weakness. I think of mothers who play the role of God from their sick-bed. Day in, day out they get their own way by appealing to their daughters' compassion and loyalty.

Looking back over his life, Cardinal Newman confessed, "I loved to choose and see my path... Pride ruled my will." The reason why many sing Newman's hymn with deep feeling is that they have to make the same confession. God does not have the place in our lives that he should. Our bias is very much in the direction of self-interest. Getting our own way is more important than the advancement of God's Kingdom. Reluctant to admit this, however, what masters of self-deception we become! We always find a good reason for behaving the way we do. Sometimes we even sanctimoniously convince ourselves that God's will coincides with what we want to do.

When the prodigal son fretted at home, wanting to be away, he probably called what he wanted 'freedom'. Out in the far country, surrounded by pretty girls, he probably called it 'pleasure'. When he lost his money he probably called it 'bad luck'. When he got down to feeding the pigs, he called himself a fool. Recalling finally his father's patient love and concern, he said, "I have sinned."

A hill-walker was impressed on noticing several circles on trees with a bullet hole dead centre. Meeting the marksman he commented on his skill. "It is easy," said the man. "I just shoot and then draw the circle!" He could not fail to score well. If we judge ourselves by our own standards, or the standards of our own social circle, we also will fare reasonably well. It is when we examine our lives in the light of the life and teaching of Jesus, his profound love for his Father and his burning desire to do God's will, that we see how far short we fall. Few can read the Sermon on the Mount or the story of the last week in Jesus' life and then tell God how highly they think of themselves.

God does not treat sin lightly. He is not to be thought of as a doting grand-parent who smooths over our rebellion and self-centredness with a benevolent 'tut-tut'. God is upset when we usurp his place and insist on living as we please.

Breakfast cups are usually inexpensive. Should our children break one, it would not be catastrophic. But suppose they were made of Dresden china. For connoisseurs in china the breakage of even one cup would be a considerable loss because of the value they place on good China. Similarly because God highly values each one of us, because he regards us as irreplaceable, he is opposed to whatever corrupts, dehumanises or breaks us.

Novelists and comedians often treat immorality, broken homes and drunkenness casually, as though they were of no great moment. But when the boy who is fast on his way to becoming an alcoholic is our son, or the brazen girl in the headlines is our daughter, or the children of the broken home our grandchildren, we see things differently. When love enters, these things are not funny.

If one of our children did not return home at night, no one in our house would go to bed. Some of the neighbours, though upset, might finally go to bed, the reason being that it is not their child. If a boy was heard singing as he staggered home, passers-by might smile and laugh, but to his parents his antics would not be funny. It is caring love that reveals the awfulness of what corrupts and defaces the image of God in people. The more concerned we are, the deeper will be our understanding of the suffering of God.

At the beginning of his letter to the Romans, Paul speaks of the characteristic vices of his day. He analyses the universality and pervasiveness of sin. He dismisses any idea that religious people are somehow exempt from its stain, and leaves us all guilty before God. Had he stopped there, he might have gone down in history as one of the great critics of the human race, another Gibbon, Swift or Voltaire, who saw history as "little more than the register of the crimes, follies and misfortunes of mankind". But the fact that "all men have sinned" was only the introduction to Paul's message. With all the genius of his mind and passion of his heart, he turns to the good news that with God there is forgiveness and the possibility of a new beginning, that God is in character like the father of the prodigal son.

> When he was yet a great way off, his father saw him, and had compassion and ran and fell on his neck and kissed him. And the son said unto him, "Father I have sinned against heaven and in thy sight and am no more worthy to be called thy son." But the father said to his servants, "Bring forth the best robe and put it on him; and put a ring on his hand and shoes on his feet; and bring hither the fatted calf and kill it; and let us eat and be merry: for this my son was dead and is alive again; he was lost and is found. (Luke 15:20-24, A.V.)

CHAPTER TWELVE

DOUBTS ABOUT FREE WILL
(Christianity and Astrology)

> "To lose one's life is a little thing, and I will have the courage when necessary. But to see the sense of this life dissipated, to see our reason for existence disappear, that is what is intolerable. A man cannot live without meaning." Albert Camus.

In our age of anxiety, the biggest anxiety of all is that life makes no sense. A report on the members of the People's Temple who took part in the Jonestown suicide pact, when 900 people died, pointed out how the majority of the members joined the sect during a period of acute depression. They had little or no sense of inner value. They joined because they longed to be part of something that was meaningful.

Not surprisingly the vacuum created by the erosion of Christian beliefs has been filled with off-beat ideas and creeds. A German philosopher of last century said, "I have the suspicion that if that strange man on the cross is finally dethroned, we will see coming out of the shadows all the old gods of lust, hate and greed, not dead but alive and riding high." More than that has come out of the shadows. There has come an upsurge in superstition, black magic and witchcraft. Any major news-stand has books on the occult, the fantastic and the weird. Astrology is also enjoying a major revival. Astrologers are regularly interviewed on radio and television. Most newspapers and magazines carry horoscopes.

For many the reading of horoscopes is a harmless bit of fun. Much that is written is little more than common sense disguised as astrology.

> "What cannot be gained near at hand may be acquired by venturing further afield."

"Fortune favours bold and enterprising Arians, so try your hardest to make those pipe-dreams come true."

Other horoscopes are so vague as to be open to various interpretations.

"Even if no major developments take place now, you can be sure that matters are moving along right lines."

Some horoscopes do, however, make more definite predictions. In December 1978 one of my youngsters read me my horoscope for 1979 (according to a magazine astrologer).

"A change of residence is definitely on the cards, spring being the likely time. You will do well financially around your birthday. Your love life in 1979 will be constantly changing. Could be you will have two relationships running at the same time."

Two years later I have to report no change of residence, no spring financial bonus and thankfully no extra-marital affair!

It is estimated that one in fifty of the adult population of Britain takes astrology seriously. *Time* magazine reported that France spends more on astrologers, fortune-tellers and clairvoyants than on scientific research, and that in Paris there are more magic-workers and clairvoyants than doctors or priests.

Speaking of the increased interest in astrology, Dr Casson, a London psychiatrist, says, "Decline in religious belief makes people avid for any guidance that seems to have a shred of plausibility and a smattering of science." He also points out how so-called civilised people, subjected as they are to the pressures and tensions of 20th century life, and often depressed by the routine of life, turn to astrology in the hope of finding the promise of better things to come.

Astrology is very old. It began around 3000 B.C. when the Babylonian priests gazed at the stars in the cloudless Mesopotamian skies and built up a great store of astronomical knowledge. By studying the movements of the sun, moon and planets, they hoped to be able to tell the time and fix the dates for sowing crops. Our modern calendar and clocks are based on their findings. Later as the priests sought the cause of the rise and fall of kings and kingdoms, storms and plagues, they believed that these also were to be found in the movements of the planets. Astrology spread from Mesopotamia to Greece and Rome. The Greeks gave the name 'Zodiac' to the heavenly track of the five visible planets or 'lamp gods' — Mercury, Venus, Mars, Jupiter and Saturn. The Romans latinised the names of the twelve constellations... Aries, Taurus, Gemini. . . .

In the ancient world astrologers were consulted before military and naval expeditions were undertaken. All important in predicting the future was the star which was rising above the horizon at the moment of a person's birth. Horoscopes were taken seriously by many in the ancient world. The Emperor Tiberius craftily executed potential rivals if their horoscopes promised fame. When the Roman Empire collapsed, so for a period did astrology. It revived with the Moorish invasion of Spain. From then until the Renaissance it enjoyed a strong following. Based on the belief that the earth was the centre round which the other heavenly bodies revolved, astrology again fell into disrepute when considerable advances were made in astronomy in the 16th and 17th centuries. The renewed interest in our day is due to the reasons mentioned, and also to the fact that our space age, science fiction made fact, has turned our attention once again to the skies.

What are we to make of astrology? There is an element of truth in it. People are affected by 'seasonal' changes (another term for planetary changes). Doctors' surgeries are busier in January and February when the sun is low in the sky. "It is the time of year,"people say. Our physical bodies and nervous systems are 'of the earth, earthy'. We have a built-in biological clock. Life having evolved out of the sea, it is not surprising that people still have in their bodies something of the rhythm of the tides as they respond to the twenty-eight day cycle of the moon. There may well be an element of truth in the old belief that seasonal or planetary changes are a contributory cause of certain mental disorders. In his book *The Lunar Effect* the psychiatrist Arnold Lieber reminds us that "Like the surface of the earth, man is about 80% water and 20% solids. I believe the gravitational force of the moon exerts an influence on the water in the human body, in you and me, as it does on the oceans of the planet.'' This is, however, a very different thing from saying that our moods and natures are predetermined by the star which was in the ascendant at our birth, or that the future can be accurately predicted by studying the stars in their courses.

The early Church denounced astrology because it denied man's free will. St Augustine gave up believing in astrology on learning that a wealthy landowner and a slave on the same estate had been born at exactly the same time. Two thousand years ago Cicero asked caustically, ''Were all those who perished at the battle of Cannae born under the same star?'' Robert Eisler, the astronomer, has called astrology, 'the stale superstitious residue of what was once a glorious attempt to understand and rationalise and explain the universe.'

In the *Dictionary of the Supernatural* Peter Underwood writes, ''Some astrologers have produced interesting predictions. Others working with the same material produce inaccurate forecasts.'' The predictions seem to be more dependent on the astrologer than on the stars. Few of the astrological predictions for 1979 were as accurate as those made by Frederick Forsyth, who did not consult the stars. In his book *The Devil's Alternative* completed in 1978 he tells how a shortage of oil prompts the Russians to use military muscle on neighbouring countries. The Americans retaliate with a grain embargo. There is a woman Prime Minister in Britain. The Shah of Iran has been deposed. There is a free-for-all in oil prices. When asked later to comment on the accuracy of his predictions, Mr Forsyth replied that the pointers were there for any observant person to see.

Long ago a Jewish writer said, ''The glory of God is to keep things hidden.'' We spoil a book when half-way through we look to the end. How much more exciting than a recording is a live television broadcast of a football match. The thrill of watching is largely dependent on the final outcome being unknown.

Likewise the secret character of the future adds considerably to the charm and excitement of living. I have difficulty understanding why people should want to consult fortune-tellers or astrologers. To remove the secret from the future would be to remove much of the joy from the present. As Al Capp said, "The man who invents a futuroid camera will have done more to make life unlivable than the man who invented the H-bomb." How dull and unexciting life would be if we knew all that lay ahead this week, the next and the next again.

If our horoscope foretold disaster would not our concern be to see if there was any way of escaping the impending calamity? This is what happened in the ancient world. Many of the ancient cults concentrated on devising means of escape from the prison house of the stars. The goddess Isis was to be praised for this above all else. "Thou unravellest even the inextricably tangled web of Fate. Thou dost alleviate the tempests of fortune and restrainest the harmful courses of the stars." The worst thing astrology did was to open the floodgates for magic to pour in. All kinds of ceremonies and formulae were devised for short-circuiting the stars, and for acquiring every sort of personal advantage. What a damaging effect this superstitious system had on Roman character! Today the concerns of astrology are still largely self-centred. They are lacking in outgoing love for one's neighbour.

In some respects it would be comforting to believe that the future depends on the movement of the stars and not on what we do or have done. If at birth the day and hour of our deaths is fixed, then with an easy mind we can drive at high speeds and smoke forty cigarettes a day. Neither would affect our decreed life-span! Looking back on life we could tell ourselves that we were fated to do what we did. We could thus escape the pain of responsibility for our mistakes. Wrong decisions and failure in human relationships were obviously due to the influence of unkindly disposed stars! Shakespeare thought otherwise. "The fault... is not in our stars, but in ourselves." In other respects however the implications of believing that all events happen exactly as decreed, and that our character is moulded by the stars are not so appealing. Maurice Hare writes,

> There was a young man who said "Damn!"
> It appears to be now that I am
> Just a being that moves
> In predestinate grooves
> Not a bus, not a bus, but a tram.

Such a fatalistic outlook would undermine moral aspiration and human effort.

The case against determinism rests not on proof, but on the basic presupposition of our everyday thinking and acting that we are free to choose between alternatives, to share or hoard, to praise or criticise, to love or hate. Although environment and heredity determine many of the pressures to which we are subject, and although seasonal influences are not to be lightly dismissed, they do not victimise us.

The idea that our destinies as individuals and nations are fixed by the stars is the very antithesis of biblical faith. Neither in the Old Testament or the New are destinies or events fixed so that what happens in time is unalterable. One of the great themes of the Old Testament is that if Israel does not change her ways, the consequences will be disastrous, but that if she does change, there will be an abundance of blessings. Jesus himself, far from accepting the established order as decreed, challenged it so sharply that those in authority wanted him silenced. His entire ministry was based on his belief that human nature could be changed, that people are responsible beings.

Determinism is not to be equated with the Christian belief in the sovereign power of God. The sovereignty of God means, not that God controls events in a direct and mechanical way, but that nothing can ultimately defeat his purposes for the world. His hold is tight enough to accomplish what he wills and intends, but loose enough to give humanity its choice.

In a glorious passage, Paul, who had plenty of unpleasant things happen to him, said to his contemporaries who were living in a star-haunted world, "I am persuaded that neither death nor life, nor angels, nor principalities, nor powers, nor things present nor things to come, nor height nor depth, nor any other creature, shall be able to separate us from the love of God..." The Greek words used for 'height' and 'depth' were astrological terms. 'Height' referred to the time a star was at its highest position in the sky, and 'depth' to the time a star was at its lowest position, waiting to rise and exert its influence for better or worse. "I am persuaded that neither the ascension of the stars, nor their declension can separate us from the love of God." For Paul this was a foundation fact of life.

Life, says the New Testament, has a point of departure, a glorious place of arrival, and a purpose big enough to bridge all the miles and minutes in between. Man's high destiny is 'to be conformed to the image of God's son'. We are called to be Christ-like, to enjoy the world God has made, and to be a channel for the love of God in that world.

Had the Church been more faithful in communicating these fundamental truths of the Christian faith, the off-beat and bizarre ideas of our time which all seek in their own way to give life significance and meaning would not have been nearly so appealing. It is at those times and in those countries where the fires of Christian faith burn low that crystal-gazing, black magic and astrology flourish.

CHAPTER THIRTEEN

DOUBTS ABOUT CHRISTIANITY
(In a World Context)
(1)

For centuries Christianity divided humanity into two camps, with Christians in the 'saved camp', and all others indiscriminately in the 'heathen camp'. The contacts between East and West were, until a hundred years ago, few and far between, and so the harm done by this view was minimal.

In the latter part of the 19th century however East and West began to meet more often. Some of the missionaries who went to the far corners of the earth made a determined effort to understand the people to whom they were sent. They studied the attempts of African tribesmen to grapple with the mysteries of the world. They studied also what the peoples of the East believed and why they believed it. They brought back with them to Britain knowledge of these other faiths. The researches of scholars such as Friedrich Max Müller further opened up for the Western mind the vast spiritual riches of the Asian religions, and their impressive insights into human problems.

In the 20th century, due to the presence of many foreigners in our country and a marked increase in foreign business trips and holidays abroad, many Britishers not only meet regularly with people of other faiths, but are also often humbled by the quality of their religious life and devotion to their faith. Dr Cave tells of travelling to the East on a crowded liner. The devotion of the Muslim passengers who each evening turned to Mecca and said their prayers contrasted sharply with the apparent irreligion of many of the 'Christian' passengers, for whom even the Sunday service was too great an interruption to their 'eating, drinking and making merry'. Professor James Robson of

Manchester who lived for many years in Arabia commented on how impressed he had been by the absence of racial prejudice in Islam, especially on the pilgrimage to Mecca. This contrasted with the racial discrimination he had witnessed in certain Christian churches.

The fact that U Thant, a devout Buddhist with a Buddhist shrine in his home, could be elected Secretary-General of the United Nations, without strong reaction from Christian countries, is a further indication of the greater openness with which those in Christian circles have come to regard other religious faiths. Our grandparents would have been most indignant that a 'pagan' should occupy such a prominent position. This exclusive, arrogant attitude is fortunately slowly disappearing.

But in the sphere of comparative religion many misunderstandings persist. Just as many were mistakenly taught that the early white settlers in America were the 'goodies' and the Indians the 'baddies', so many were led to believe that whereas the Crusaders were educated, dedicated, chivalrous men, the Muslims were all illiterate brutes and barbarous infidels. Now admittedly some of the fanatical and power obsessed caliphs who offered conquered tribes the choice of conversion or death, were barbarous, power-mad characters, but so too were many of the Crusaders. It was the Crusaders and not the Saracens who boasted that, when they first took Jerusalem, the blood of the infidels, including wives and children, flowed through the streets as deep as the horses' stirrups.

To judge Islam or any other faith by its worst representatives is unfair. A religion ought to judged by its best representatives and by what at best it stands for. Mohammed's concern was to cleanse the imperial religion of idolatry and star-worship. Islam, indeed, has been called the Arabian Protestantism of the 7th century. Though he rejected current theories about the divinity of Jesus, he did not reject Jesus himself. He regarded him as a kind of supreme example of what is meant by 'submission to God' (the meaning of the word Islam). Mohammed's own faith was in a merciful, compassionate God. "He is Allah, the Creator, the Maker, the Fashioner. Whatever is in the heavens and the earth declares his glory. He is the Mighty and the Wise." Looking forward to the day when all who shared a common belief in God would exist together in peace, the prophet is reported to have said to a deputation of Christians, "Conduct your services here in the mosque. It is a place consecrated to God." Although some of his followers later used force against outsiders, Mohammed regarded tolerance as a fundamental virtue.

The Old Testament reminds us how Abraham was the friend of God and how the Psalmist through his faith in God had lost his fear of death. We would not say that these Jews were deceived because they were not Christians. Nor ought we to give the impression that those in other religions who have earnestly sought after religious truth and longed for fellowship with God have been totally deceived. To imply this, or to say that God did not speak to the world through men like Socrates, Plato, Buddha, Confucius and Mohammed is spiritual arrogance of the worst kind.

When Moses learned that 'unauthorised' persons were prophesying, his reply was: "Are you jealous for my sake? Would that all the Lord's people were prophets, that the Lord would put his spirit upon them!" Jesus said much the same to his followers when they complained about the activities of others who were not of their circle. Surely we ought to rejoice that knowledge of God extends beyond what our forefathers supposed. We ought to welcome light wherever it shines. Light is light and it is blasphemy to call it darkness.

The New Testament teaches that there is a Light which enlightens every man, that God has never left himself without a witness, that through many inspired people God has spoken to the human race. Gautama Buddha's eightfold path, designed to help people to give up bad desires is a noble one–right views, right resolve, right speech, right activity, right livelihood (living), right endeavour, right mindfulness and right rapture (meditation). In the social teaching of Confucius there is also much that is admirable. Confucius' emphasis on the sacredness of work, the need for education, the importance of loyalty and good manners in young people, and what he called the 'noble virtues'–dignity, generosity, mercy, tolerance and sincerity–built enduring strength into Chinese family life and character. Confucius' prime concern was with people and the problems of people living in community. Although he seems to have believed in a Supreme God, he never concerned himself with philosophical and theological questions concerning the origin of life or the meaning of existence, questions which in the 6th century B.C. were preoccupying many thinkers in India and the Middle East.

There are moral maxims of the Buddha which also closely correspond with those of Jesus. In the Sermon on the Mount Jesus condemned those who see the speck in their brother's eye, but fail to notice the log in their own. Buddhism says, "To see another's fault is easy: to see one's own is hard. Men winnow the faults of others like chaff; their own they hide as a crafty gambler hides a losing throw." When cursed, said Jesus, we are not to curse back. In passage after passage, Buddhism says the same.

> Worse is he, who when reviled, reviles again;
> He who when reviled doth not revile again
> A two-fold victory wins.

In the Dhammapada, a kind of Buddhist Psalter, one hymn reads, "Overcome anger by not growing angry. Never does hatred cease by hating." Jesus would have said Amen to that, as he would to most of Mohammed's exhortations to his followers shortly before the prophet's death. "Be kind to the poor. Give the labourer his wages before the sweat of his brow has dried. You are all members of one brotherhood..."

There are, however, also differences between the ethical teaching of Jesus and the moral traditions of other faiths. Islam and Christianity differ markedly in their teaching about marriage, Buddhism and Christianity in their teaching about the possibility of being forgiven, Hinduism and Christianity in their thinking about class and caste. When Bernard Shaw's *Pygmalion* was staged in New Delhi, more progressive Indians pointed out that a Hindu version would be unthinkable. The Cockney flower girl would be untouchable and never allowed to enter the house of the Brahmin Henry Higgins. Christianity, in belief, if not always in practice, is opposed to such a rigid division of society into classes or castes. "There is no such thing as Jew and Greek, slave and freeman, male and female; for you are all one person in Christ Jesus."

Whereas Confucius taught that love is to be reserved for friends, and that enemies deserve only justice, Jesus taught that we should also love our enemies, feeding them when hungry, helping them when in need. For Confucius, as for Hillel, the first century Jewish Rabbi, the governing principle was, "What I do not wish others to do to me, that also I wish not to do to them." Jesus, aware that little gets accomplished by purely negative virtue, by refraining from hurting others, gave a more positive summary. "Always treat others as you would like them to treat you." The attitude which says, "I must not harm people" is far removed from that which says, "I must do my best to help others."

As we shall see in the next chapter, it is, however, in the sphere of philosophical and theological thought that the major differences occur between the world religions.

CHAPTER FOURTEEN

DOUBTS ABOUT CHRISTIANITY
(In a World Context)
(2)

In Senegal, a predominantly Islamic West African country, Muslims recently joined with Christians in conducting a programme of social and economic development for two hundred Muslims living in a drought-stricken area. The programme was sponsored by the Y.M.C.A. and it involved a Jewish technical agency. When people read of such commendable interreligious approaches to helping the disadvantaged, or of people of different faiths cooperating to promote greater peace and justice in the world, some wonder whether the solution to the problem of the world's religions might not be to merge the best elements from the various traditions, to create an 'Esperanto' world faith. Those who advocate such an approach, often with the best of intentions, fail to realise, however, just how varied are the underlying philosophies of some of the major world faiths. A common superficial morality might be feasible, but not a common theology. There is for example no way of reconciling the Buddha's denial of the existence of a Supreme God, or his belief that life is a penalty and a thing of sorrow, with the teaching of Christianity.

There is no way either of reconciling the law of Karma with the teaching of Jesus. According to the law of Karma we are all endlessly reborn. The cow that we see in the field or the monkey in the zoo may be our great-aunt. Because Westerners tend to interpret reincarnation with certain modifications, they often do not realise just how depressing psychologically the belief is. One of these modifications is that those who do well in their present life will be reborn to a better life so that in each new reincarnation we receive the just punishment or reward for evil or good done in some previous existence. If those who have struggled up through lower forms of life sin gravely, they will have to atone for their misdeeds when life is over, perhaps by taking the form of a pig or reptile. Orthodox Hinduism however denies this, insisting that the circumstances of rebirth are purely accidental and bear no relation to virtue. A doctor may become a snake for no reason except that the wheel of life (a national symbol on the flag of India) is going round and round inexorably; and since everyone is on it, he is bound sometimes to be up and sometimes down. Gautama Buddha is said to have lived through five hundred and thirty lives before reaching the status of the Enlightened One. (Just as Christ means the Anointed One, so the word Buddha means the Enlightened One.)

The other modification of reincarnation which makes it slightly more attractive is that many in the West assume that personality and identity are retained in successive rebirths. Examples are sometimes quoted of people apparently remembering a former life or lives, or of people retaining skills acquired in some previous existence. Orthodox Hindus do not, however, believe this. What survives, they say, is life energy, not personality. Buddhist philosophers stress that there can be no question of personal immortality, or eternal life with a personal God.

The supreme quest of Buddhist thought and piety is the quest for liberation (moksha) from the endless cycle of rebirth (the wheel of samsara). Escape from the dismal human condition involves not only giving up bad desires, but also good desires. "Crush your desires so that you reach a stage when you no longer want to exist or be reborn." "Happy are those who hold nothing in the world dear." Christianity on the other hand is concerned that our desires should be enlarged and ennobled, that we should hold dear the things Jesus held dear.

The goal of life for the Buddhist is Nirvana. This has often mistakenly been equated with the Christian concept of heaven. But in Buddhism there is neither heaven nor God, only final nothingness for those fortunate enough to attain total indifference or detachment. Nirvana signifies the ending of all desire, all love and hatred, the extinction of individuality and absorption into nothingness. The peace of Nirvana is the peace of not-being, the peace of a candle that has been blown out. Christianity sees the goal of life differently. In the words of Dorothy Sayers, "God does not desire the absorption of the many into the One. His love is anxiously directed to confirm each individual in his own identity, so that the nearer it draws to him, the more truly it becomes its unique and personal self."

Professor Arthur Gossip, whose wife died prematurely, dedicated one of his books years later to her: "To my wife, now a long time in the Father's house." Pandit Nehru also dedicated one of his books to his late wife: "To Kamala who is no more." What a world of difference between these two inscriptions, the difference between a faith that quickens the human heart, and a faith which has no Risen Lord to say, "Because I live you shall live also... In my Father's house are many mansions. I go to prepare a place for you."

One of my teachers, Dr Van Dusen, told of a remarkable institution on the outskirts of Hong Kong which he had once visited. It was called the 'Buddhist Christian Institute'. It was a retreat or study centre where Buddhists, especially Buddhist priests who wanted to know more about Christianity, could go and live and study and reflect. Some returned to their Buddhist vocations, but others stayed on to prepare for the Christian ministry. The building was in the style of a typical Buddhist monastery. At the Institute the self-discipline so characteristic of Buddhist meditation was practised, a self-discipline which would make Christian prayer for many Westerners much more profound than the usual "God bless..." or "Jesus tender shepherd hear me..." At the centre of the building there was a chapel with a simple altar. Above the altar was a carved open lotus lily, the Buddhist symbol of unfolding truth. Above the lily hung a cross signifying that Christianity does not seek to destroy other faiths, but to complete them.

An interesting characteristic of our day is that many in the West are more interested in studying the religions of the East than in learning about the faith that has moulded Western civilisation. How ignorant they often are of the Christan faith!

In practice their study of Buddhism and Hinduism or any other Eastern religion rarely includes the spiritual disciplines advocated by these religions. A lady, more honest than many, frankly confessed of her spiritual quest, "Since I neither adopted the Four Noble Truths nor trod the Noble Eightfold Path, my alleged sympathy with Hinduism and Buddhism was more a protest than a reasoned belief." Vital religious faith involves the commitment of heart, mind, soul and strength. The easy-going tolerance which can give assent to any and every point of view, which maintains that all religions are equally true, is really a form of indifference that is not far removed from the universal scepticism which would dismiss all faith as an illusion.

Radhakrishnan, a vice-President of India, a charming and scholarly Hindu, once said, partly in derision, "Christians are ordinary people who make extraordinary claims." That describes exactly what we are and the dilemma which faces the Church in the sphere of comparative religion. It is not easy to make the extraordinary claims that we do make for Jesus and at the same time not offend those of other faiths. To be aware of our many shortcomings as Christians, and to be alert to the good that God stores in every life, and at the same time make extraordinary claims for our faith is not easy. But amiability does not release us from the compulsion of stating what we believe, that by his coming into the world Jesus corrected, clarified and fulfilled, not only the Jewish understanding of God, man and life, but also the Buddhist's and Hindu's understanding of these things.

Nor do good manners free us from the compulsion to point out that there is no other religion which fills the words 'God', 'Man' and 'Life' with such glorious meaning as does Christianity. Jesus taught people to think of God as infinitely compassionate and concerned. He likened him to a shepherd, prepared to risk all to find one lost sheep, to a loving, forgiving Father running down the road, with tears in his eyes, to welcome home a lad who had brought shame on the family name. There is no parallel to this in the other religions of the world. How cold by comparison is Confucius' concept of Tien; how impersonal the many-headed Brahma of Hinduism!

No other person ever had such a high regard for humanity

as Jesus had. Among the many differences between the two eras, B.C. and A.D., none is as remarkable as this difference in the accepted estimate of man. Jesus taught that human souls are not manufactured and distributed through some celestial Woolworth's but are in fact infinitely valuable, each one greatly loved by God.

There is also no other religion that produces such fulness of life for the individual and society as Christianity does, not as Christianity is often conceived and practised, but as Jesus taught and lived it. How unchristian is the feverish and hunted tempo of life in the so-called Christian West, which is constantly fabricating new needs and desires! Human nature is so constituted that it is never fulfilled so long as it is turned in on itself, so long as it is selfishly preoccupied with things and the satisfying of its own self-centred desires.

Gandhi, who fought so valiantly for the outcasts of India, admired Jesus more than anyone else. The two pictures that hung in his very simple living room were both of Jesus, one of him washing the disciples' feet, the other of him hanging on the Cross saying, "Father forgive them, they don't know what they are doing." Again how great is the gulf between Christianity as Jesus practised it and as we practise it! It is significant that when Mahatma Gandhi was assassinated, his fellow Hindus did not liken him to any of their gods. They likened him to Christ. They could think of nothing higher to say of him. At his funeral, the hymn which was sung by those who knew it was Gandhi's favourite, "When I survey the wondrous Cross."

Throughout the world today most people unwittingly assume that Jesus is the ideal man, or at least the man who of all men comes nearest to that ideal. Confucius, Moses, Mohammed, Buddha or Gandhi, or some other figure of another faith might be pointed to as standing up reasonably well by comparison, but the comparison in the last resort is with one who does not really have any rival, Jesus of Nazareth.

It is mistaken to say that any Christian is better than any Hindu. On the other hand I am persuaded that faith in Christ is better than faith in Krishna because it leads the believer to a deeper understanding of God and man; and, if practised, it makes him more human. This being so, a compulsion is laid on

Christians to spread love and truth, Christian faith and hope.

People like Aggrey of Africa, Kagawa of Japan, Sadhu Sundar Singh and D.T. Niles of India, Charles Malik of the Lebanon, Martin Luther King of America and many others remind us how Christianity, at its finest, meets the needs of people of every race and clime. There is a universal appeal about the central character of the centuries.

CHAPTER FIFTEEN

DOUBTS ABOUT THE COMMANDMENTS

"In medicine there is no 'always' and no 'never'." So said a professor of medicine. He could recall several patients who he had thought would die within days but who had lived for years. Other patients who he had been certain would recover, had died in his care. Experience had taught him that medical rules are not universally valid. Doctors ought therefore to avoid the words *always* and *never*. It's a much-needed reminder. Yet the last thing he intended was that the doctors he was addressing should there and then forget the rules they had been taught. He knew that though there are exceptional cases, yet the medical rules do usually apply.

Like the professor, many who advocate the new morality have drawn our attention to the fact that the ancient prohibitions of the Mosaic law do not always apply. Extreme situations can arise where the demands of Christian love conflict with the commandments; situations where it is permissible to kill, commit adultery or bear false witness.

Was not Dietrich Bonhoeffer justified in participating in the plot to kill Hitler who was causing such suffering throughout Europe? And those French mothers, faced with the alternative of having their husbands brutally tortured or giving their bodies to a Nazi officer, were they not justified in committing adultery? What also of those brave folk in the underground movement? Are we not right to call the lies which love prompted them to tell 'white lies'? Circumstances do alter cases.

Life in community can give rise to *extreme* situations where the demands of love conflict with the commandments. The advocates of situational ethics and some modern novelists delight in seizing on such exceptional cases. They pose and seek to answer the question, how people with divided loyalties ought to act in some complex situation.

The substitution of love for rules and the particular for the general constitutes the thrust of the new morality. In *Honest to God* Bishop Robinson describes the new morality thus. "It is a radical ethic of the situation with nothing prescribed except love." At its finest the new morality is in keeping with the New Testament. Love, in the sense of intelligent caring, was for Jesus the fulfilment of the moral law. "You ought to care for one another as I have cared for you." Jesus knew that a life dominated by law and not tempered by love becomes mechanical, hard and unyielding. It is observant of the letter of the law, but neglectful of the spirit. It will go the mile of compulsion but not the second mile of compassion. The legalistic outlook tends to be cold, but Christ-like caring is always warm.

The element of truth in the new morality–that the particular situation has to be considered and that love is the standard and ideal of the moral life–tends to obscure the dangers. Those attracted by it often mistakenly conclude that since rules cannot cover all the complex situations in which people find themselves and that since you cannot use the words 'always' and 'never,' the rules ought to be abandoned. Though this might just be possible in a society of angels, it is surely obvious that men are not angels.

We hear often of the evangelical mission of the Church. Perhaps we should hear oftener of the unangelic mission of the church, for the Church's mission is one conducted by unangelic people to others equally unangelic. If people always exercised self-control and acted unselfishly and honestly, external restraints might not be necessary, but people are far from being perfect. If all laws were abolished, to what fearful lengths many of us might go when roused?

Shortly after the Russian Revolution, the communists decided to do away with what they contemptuously described as 'bourgeois morality'. Tired of your wife, you left her and lived with the next woman you fancied. No legal contract was required. So colossal were the problems created, however, that gradually the more responsible Russian leaders realised that moral laws were essential to prevent society from disintegrating. Where there is no respect for law and order, barbarism takes over.

A Spanish story tells of a gypsy who went to confession. When asked by the priest if he knew the Ten Commandments, the gypsy answered, "Well, Father, it is this way. I was going to learn them, but I heard talk that they were soon going to do away with them." Lawlessness is one of our greatest problems today. Armed hold-ups, brutal assaults and murders are almost daily occurrences. What an alarming increase there has also been in the number of quiet thieves who steal from shops, employers and the government. Innumerable babies are being conceived out of wedlock. Our V.D. clinics can scarcely cope.

Every language has its irregular verbs and spellings. One does not however on this account refrain from first teaching children the rules and the regular verbs and spellings. In Britain we have what is called common law. But because there are borderline cases which do not fit any prescribed pattern, we also have case law. Lawyers are, I am sure, grateful that not all law is case law, that on most occasions there are great general principles to guide their thinking.

"In my callow youth," wrote Dr Fosdick, "I reached the conclusion that we had so far spiritually progressed that we could centre all our attention on Paul's statement, 'Love is the fulfilling of the law' and that we need no longer stress the negative, 'Thou shalt not'. I take it back now. I know human life better." Like Dr Fosdick I sometimes wish that the commandments, "You shall not steal;" "You shall not kill;" "You shall not commit adultery," were exhibited in every shopping centre, school and church. The general principle is far more important than the exceptional or extreme case.

We need moral laws which forbid, require and permit, which guide us as to what we must do, may do or must not do. Otherwise we would often be confused as to how to act and how to apply Christian love. A healthy conscience has a positive and a negative side. The positive side is constructive: "You shall do this." The negative side is prohibitive: "You shall not do this." Paul regarded the life and teaching of Jesus as providing the ideal pattern for the good life. Wanting his readers to be generous, he reminded them of one who though he was rich, yet for their sakes became poor. Wanting them to be humble, he reminded them of him who though he was divine by nature laid aside his glory to become a servant. Thus Paul sought to train positively the consciences of the early Christians.

But Paul, fearful of anarchy, also asked them to respect the Ten Commandments and the laws of the state. Paul knew that though some of his contemporaries could be trusted to impose moral restraints on themselves, others needed to have restraints imposed, lest they infringe the rights of their neighbours. Laws cannot reform the heart. But thank God they can restrain the heartless until they change their mind and heart. Roman Law was something the Roman citizen revered. Even conquered tribes learned a new sense of security when they put themselves under the justice of Roman law. The basic aim of laws and commandments is not to forbid, but to preserve and enlarge the freedom and well-being of all. As someone has rightly said, "That does not deserve the name of confinement which hedges us from bogs and precipices." Far from being angels, are we not in fact such cunning creatures that, having done what inclination dictated, we seek to justify our conduct? Jumping off a bus without paying, we try to save face by saying, "People on a crowded bus ought not to have to pay!" Travelling at 45 m.p.h. in a 30 m.p.h. zone, we convince ourselves that the road ought to have a 40 m.p.h. limit.

More anxious to justify their conduct than regulate it, many are attracted by the new morality, where the only absolute is love, for this complex quality can be made to mean almost anything they want. It can disguise prudent selfishness, greed, even lust. Because dishonesty can thus degrade love, love as the absolute must be closely linked with attributes like honour and loyalty. Love needs such supports and safeguards. Surely one of the finest couplets which chivalry ever inspired reads,

> "I could not love thee, dear, so much.
> Lov'd I not honour more."

Love often inspires sacrificial conduct which no law can demand. Though in exceptional cases love may have to act contrary to the law, love, if it is to be Christ-like, will always have the highest respect for the law.

CHAPTER SIXTEEN
DOUBTS ABOUT THE CHURCH

Both from pulpit and pew the Church comes in for severe criticism. We all know what is wrong with the Church. "It is full of hypocrites... It is hopelessly old-fashioned... It speaks *grandioso* on minor themes and *sotto voce*–with a little voice–on major issues... It is not sufficiently involved in the heartache of modern society..." Such disparaging statements about the Church are nothing new. They have been levelled against the Church in almost every age. The church has needed her reformers, men like Martin Luther, John Wesley, General Booth and Pope John XXIII to right her when she wandered from Christ's way. That she has often done so, few would deny.

But that is not the whole story of the Church, though often her critics stop there. Although she has persecuted her reformers and saints, we should remember that it was the Church which produced them. Though the Church in Germany failed in any unified protest against Nazism, the greatest measure of protest that did come, came from a small group within the institutional Church. However imperfect some of her members are, others have proven themselves to be the salt of the earth. The Church has made the world a better place. To tour the ruins of some ancient city is to see the remains of many buildings of which the counterparts may be found in a modern city — theatres, sports arenas, schools. But among these ruins will be found no trace of an orphanage, hospital or asylum for the mentally ill, or a home for the aged. Ancient civilisations made little or no provision for those most in need. The first hospitals were sponsored and run by the Church. The honoured place occupied by the child in society stemmed from the Church's insistence that children ought not to be used as money-making tools, that they have a right to an adequate childhood without sweat-shop labour. The caring concern of the Church prompted governments into deeper concern for needy humanity. The Church's money has also been the financial framework and its members the flesh and sinews of a great deal of charitable work in our own land and overseas. Healing waters have flowed from the Church for the renewal of the life of man. People sometimes say, ''I will have nothing more to do with the Church. You see that minister or elder or that Mrs Jones who is in her pew every Sunday . . .'' There then follows a list of the minister's, elder's or Mrs Jones' shortcomings. Irrespective of whether what they say is true, that is not a valid reason for having nothing more to do with the Church. What would we think of someone who said, ''Because policemen have on occasions been caught shoplifting or ill-treating prisoners, I will have nothing more to do with the police''; or the person who said, ''I am finished with Chopin because the girl next door makes such a fearful mess of playing his Nocturnes''? Yet how many say, ''I will have nothing more to do with Christianity because the Rev. Mr Smith or Mrs Jones makes such a mess of living the Christian life.''

Few, if any, think of trees in terms of stunted shrubs, but rather in terms of majestic oaks. So we ought to judge the Church, not by its unworthy members, but by those fine folk who are not only in their pews on Sundays, but who do honestly try to be good neighbours, who give generously of their time to help run youth and community organisations, who exert a Christ-like influence on business and public opinion, on community and political affairs, who are more concerned about poverty and prejudice than premium bonds. We ought also to judge the Church as we do other institutions by what at best the Church stands for and seeks to accomplish.

On the occasion of the dedication of the first Jewish temple Solomon prayed, ''Behold heaven and the highest heaven cannot contain thee; how much less this house that I have built.'' Solomon simply hoped that the church he had built might convey a faint whisper of God's majesty and power, for beauty is a divine whisper of God's majesty speaking to something in us deeper than reason, in language too deep for words. The poet who wrote the Book of Job felt this way about the beauty of the natural world, the movement of the wind and the sea, the silent movement of the stars and the seasons. ''These,'' he said, ''are the outskirts of his ways." The Church helps preserve the dimension of depth and mystery that there is to beauty, truth and life itself.

Little men speak glibly of human knowledge, but wise men know that what we hear is but a whisper of divine truth. On Isaac Newton's tomb his admirers chiselled the boastful words,

> Nature and Nature's laws lay hid in night:
> God said, "Let Newton be!" and all was light.

Newton would have cringed had he read that. He was aware of how much he did not know. He said once that he was like a little child picking up a few pebbles on the seashore while around him lay the great ocean of truth undiscovered. Beyond our careful sciences and clever 'ologies'—geology, anthropology, biology, zoology—there is mystery. Beyond the height of the sky and the depth of the human mind, beyond our neon-lighted civilisation and our biochemical explanations there is also mystery, but a mystery at the heart of which, as the Church knows, there is Christ-like love.

Man's spirit cries out for that which a larder full of good food and a wardrobe full of expensive clothes cannot provide. Expensive houses and cars, winter-skiing holidays and summer cruises to get away from the mad buzz of the world, though good and enjoyable in themselves, will not ultimately satisfy. They are in fact little more than the human version of a dog's longing for a bigger bone or a horse's longing to be rid of the flies. Though Jesus was attuned to man's need for bread, he was also attuned to man's deep hunger for such intangible things as beauty, truth, freedom and God. I believe in the Church also because she ministers to these deep hungers. She insists on a religious view of the world and human life. She lifts our ponderous earth to her ear, as we would lift a shell, and hears the roll of the eternal sea.

In his book *Rain upon Godshill*, J.B. Priestley reminds us of what the Church contributes to our 'not being lost in the universe'.

> People like my parents, to use their matchless phrase, attended places of worship. Now that I see the old phrase with a fresh eye, I see also how astonishing it is. Places of worship. How much we have lost, we of the younger generation by having no places of worship! Perhaps

this new world must remain desolate at heart until it achieves new places of worship. Then the spirit of man will come home again to the universe. What is certain is that the absence of church or chapel from these young people's lives, has vastly increased their sense of detachment and their feeling of loneliness.

One night Lord Tennyson and a friend were discussing what each sought to get out of life. The friend said, "I ask that I should leave the world a better place than when I found it." Tennyson responded, "And I ask that I should have a new and bigger vision of God." How important are those hours when we are given a vision of God and the purposes of God, when we are helped to see life in perspective, a drama played out, not against two dates on a tombstone, but against an eternal background, for many see little or nothing in life worth living for. Each day has become a matter of putting in time, seeking at night some little dash of entertainment to stall off the awful boredom.

Prisoners of war, confined for years behind barbed wire fences, sometimes developed what was called barbed wire sickness. The doctors were helpless, because there was no physical cause. The sickness stemmed from the unnatural limitations of their boundaries. There could be no cure until they were freed from such limitations. Is it not similar with the spiritual sickness of our time? Does not the prevalent feeling of aimlessness and boredom stem from man's denial that he is an eternal creature, and from his acceptance of this world's boundaries as final? I thank God that our landscape is dotted with church spires, reminding people of the eternal dimension to life, and of a more excellent way than the world's way.

For more than a decade Dr Andrei Sakharov, the distinguished Russian physicist, has fearlessly condemned the treatment meted out in Russia to dissidents, including his close friend Solzhenitsyn. Week after week he has stood vigil outside the Moscow law-courts, pleading for greater freedom and more just trials. What courage it takes to stand out for truths that are considered unpatriotic. During an interview with a Swedish radio commentator, the interviewer drew Dr Sakharov's attention to the fact that despite his years of protesting, the situation in Russia was really no better. Why continue then to make himself so unpopular with the Russian authorities? To this he replied, "You always need to make ideals clear. You always have to be aware of them, even if there is no direct path to their realisation. Were there no ideals there would be no hope whatsoever. Then everything would be hopelessness, darkness, a blind alley."

At the height of the United States involvement in South-East Asia, a group of ministers urged Henry Kissinger to withdraw U.S. troops. Mr Kissinger, hounding them on the complexities of such a proposal, asked, "How would you get the boys out of Vietnam?" To which one of the ministers, Bill Coffin, turning to the Book of Amos, responded, "Mr Kissinger, our job is to proclaim that 'justice must roll down like waters, and righteousness like a mighty stream.' Your job is to work out the details of the irrigation system!" Despite all her stuttering and stammering, the Church does keep reminding politicians and those who elect them of those truths and ideals without which there is no hope of a better future.

Martin Luther once said that human problems began when mankind became *incurvatus in se*, bent inwards towards itself. In more modern jargon, contemporary psychiatrists say much the same thing. Even the worship of the sun would be a more wholesome thing than man's worship of himself! The impulses which drive many today are predominantly selfish. We all tend to make ourselves the centre of the universe, pushing away centrifugally from the centre everything that impedes our free-wheeling. Get what you can as quickly as you can, enjoy it while you are able, and let your neighbour take care of himself. If sacrifices are to be made, let others make them. It was much the same in Jesus' day and how it saddened him. He saw people capable of being the glory of the universe, yet content with being its shame. He sought to drive them out of their miserable selfish ways and to enlarge the horizons of their concern. He called on them to love God by loving their neighbours, to serve God by serving his other children, to go the second mile, to be a just and caring community. I believe in the Church because she keeps issuing this challenge of service in a selfish world.

The Church is also precious because she recalls, interprets, celebrates and communicates the greatest story ever told, the story of the birth, life, death and resurrection of Jesus, the story of how God stood once in our shoes. Frederick Buechner recalls a fable which the Hindu saint Ramakrishna once told of a motherless tiger cub that was adopted by goats and brought up to copy their ways, eat their food and in general believe he was a goat. Then one day a king tiger came along. The goats scattered but the young tiger stayed, bleating nervously and nibbling at the grass. The king tiger took him to a pool and forced him to look at their reflections side by side, and then draw his own conclusions. He next offered the young tiger his first piece of raw meat. At first the young tiger recoiled. The taste was unfamiliar. But then as he ate, he began to feel his whole body responding. Gradually the truth became clear. He was not a goat but a tiger. Digging his claws into the ground, the young tiger raised his head high and let out an exultant roar.

We hear a great deal today about man's search for his own identity. Is not this a modern way of expressing the same truth as Ramakrishna's fable? We are not the people God hoped we would be. If the tiger who thinks he is a goat could just settle down and be quite content living as a goat, he would have no problems. But fortunately there is still enough of the tiger in us, to make us discontented with our goathood. Memory, regret, longing, hope, anticipation–these make us misfits in a goat environment. Essentially we have an ideal which transcends such an environment. We have immortal longings, higher hungers. We eat succulent grasses but they never really fill us. We bleat well enough but deep down there is the suspicion that we were made for roaring. Jesus we could liken to the king tiger. Glancing up from our grazing, from our preoccupation with fame and fortune, power and pleasure, we see in Jesus what a human being really looks like, man as God intended him to be. We see the fulfilment of the aspirations and ideals which secretly attract us.

At so many points Jesus satisfies our deepest needs. Our inability to find fulfilment in material things fits in with his teaching about God in whose fellowship and service we were made to find deep satisfaction. Our experience of the strange self-defeating quality of selfishness fits in with Jesus' call to fulfil our lives in causes greater than our own. Our inescapable sense of missing the mark, of not being the kind of people we ought to be, fits in with Jesus' own demonstration, not only of the kind of life we were meant for, but of the possibility of forgiveness and a new beginning. His promise that he will be with us until the end of time and that he will grant us strength to cope fits in with the considerable demands the Christian way of life can make on us. How wonderfully the fact of Christ and the facts of life elucidate and interpret one another!

Many long for the renewal of genuine Christianity in our land, for what they significantly call the birth of a 'new spirit' in man. But many fail to realise that this will only come about through a renewal of the life of the Church and the recovery of her essential message. Seeing only the Church's faults and failures, they make these an excuse for washing their hands of the Church. They forget that just as education and justice would not last long without schools and law-courts, Christian faith and values will not last long without some kind of organised Church. There is no way of carrying forward human beliefs and patterns of behaviour from one human life or generation to the next, other than by means of communities organised as institutions. Professor John Foster put it forcibly, "Christianity as a disembodied influence would not long survive the passing of the Body, the Church. Diffused idealism would soon only be a fragrance on the breeze. Indeed it might only be a smell." Had it not been for the institutional Church we today would know nothing of Jesus. The question is not whether we will have an organised Church, but what kind of organised Church we are to have.

If we liken the Church to a tree then our need is to do with it what Jesus suggested we should do with a bulky vine. We must prune it and get rid of its dead wood, so that it may become more fruitful. To root it out would be an awful mistake. The world is bad enough with the Church. Without the Church the present darkness would be remembered as a light to be coveted. In an article which Bernard Shaw once wrote for 'The St Martin Review' he said that if ever people found themselves deprived of churches, they would find that they had been deprived of a necessity of life, and the want would somehow have to be supplied. Despite her many failures, the Church occupies central place in God's scheme of things.

CHAPTER SEVENTEEN

DOUBTS ABOUT THE MINISTRY AND LAITY

Paul spoke of the Church as the "body of Christ". The business world was quick to seize on this analogy. They borrowed from the church the idea of corporation, 'corpus' being the Latin word for body. They used the word corporation to describe a large group of people working as one to achieve a stated purpose. The people who make up corporations, whether city or industrial, contribute their individual skills to a task too great for anyone to accomplish alone. Such is the role of the Church. Her task, that of establishing God's kingdom on earth, is one that is too great for any one person or group to accomplish. Every member of the body, archbishop and bus-driver, graduate and grandmother, has the same basic vocation.

It is unfortunate that the word 'minister' often conjures up visions of Roman collars and Geneva gowns. Its continued application only to the clergy perpetuates the mistaken assumption that there is only one person within the congregation who ministers. Concerned as I was about this denial of the equality of our calling as Christians, I was heartened to see on the notice board of an American Presbyterian Church the words,

Ministers . . . . All members of Center Church
Teaching Elder . . . . John C. Peterson.

Here was a 'team ministry' where the difference between clergy and laity was one of function rather than status. And of course to be consistent 'laity' like 'ministry' should apply to all Christians. The Greek word 'laos' is used in the New Testament to mean the 'the whole people of God.'

A denominational form posed the question, "How many ministers are there in your congregation?" How the statistics must have been warped by one minister writing the figure 600 in the allotted space! Was he not justified? In naming ministers we cannot possibly stop after listing Moses, Aaron, Peter and a long line of ordained clergy. I would want for example to include people like the 'priestly' pensioner who refreshed me recently with her wise words of encouragement and understanding. She ministered to me by helping me to see a little future over the wall of an apparently dead-end street.

In most organisations a distinction ultimately develops, however, between ordinary members and those who make their living by working full time for an organisation. Even the most egalitarian groups find that as the membership increases, someone full-time has to be appointed to help promote their goals. The Church was no exception. The New Testament makes no clear distinction between the various officials within the Church. Yet as the Church grew, it was found to be necessary to set aside certain individuals to devote their full-time energies to the on-going life of the Church, and to have special responsibility for the administration of the sacraments, the instruction of new members and the preaching of the gospel. Later still the Church decided that only 'professionals' were to be allowed to carry out those functions which were regarded as particularly sacred and crucial to the life of the Church.

This created a cleavage between ministers and laity which developed until the point was reached when it was stated in a papal encyclical that "The Church is essentially an unequal society, that is to say, a society composed of two categories of persons, pastors and flock... and these categories are so distinct in themselves that in the pastoral body alone reside the necessary right and authority to guide and direct all members... As for the multitude it has no other right than that of allowing itself to be led, and as a docile flock, to follow its shepherds."

Monasticism, which seems to have started partly as a protest against clerical centralisation, very quickly made the same mistake. The monks became in some ways a spiritual aristocracy in the midst of an unenlightened and spiritually inferior majority. Martin Luther protested against this idea of there being a superior priestly caste. He emphasised the 'priesthood of all believers'. All who sought to maintain and enrich human life were, he believed, consecrated priests. But today there is still an insidious clericalism in so much church life. The sharp distinction between the clergy and the laity, the sacred and the secular, persists.

Not surprisingly the laity concluded that since the sacred and the spiritual were the clergy's special remit, ministers and priests ought not to get involved in such 'profane' things as economic or political matters. These were the concern of the laity.

In our day, ministers and lay people respect each other so long as each minds its own business. But they often get 'uptight' when the other group starts meddling in their affairs. Some ministers become anxious when lay people become too insistent about participating in the conduct of worship. A stumbling block in the proposed basis of union of the Church of Scotland with the Congregational Church was that certain congregational laymen were allowed to consecrate the elements at communion. That was not acceptable to many Church of Scotland ministers.

Likewise many lay people resent ministers interfering in their affairs. They can become more than a little hostile when the clergy lead protest marches on social issues, or question the wisdom of government policies or technological innovations. When Bishop Montefiore, who was concerned about noise abatement, went to America to argue the case against supersonic flights, he was told by a Member of Parliament that he would have been better employed giving his attention to 'spiritual' matters rather than getting involved in 'political sky-piloting'. Without going into arguments for or against 'Concorde', I feel the same charge would not have been levelled against him, had he supported the 'Concorde' programme. When ministers criticise policies people believe in, that is the Church meddling in politics. When on the other hand they voice the political views that people want to hear, that is not meddling in politics!

The Church has reason to be proud of its educated ministry. It rightly requires of all candidates for the ministry a good education, a knowledge of and insight into Biblical criticism, systematic theology and Church history. But the layman may well ask whether this is enough, whether the Church has not in fact failed to equip her ministers to conduct services that ar meaningful to the working man, and to speak in everyday language of the relevance of the Christian faith to contemporary life. God, Jesus and the gospel are the same "yesterday, today and forever", but the language we use to speak of them cannot be the same.

The clergy are equally justified in pointing out that for the most part the laity have failed to fulfil their half of the division of labour. They have failed to grasp that God is as concerned about what goes on in the community as he is with what goes on in Church. As Dr George Macleod pointed out, "Perhaps the most disturbing element about the parable of the Last Judgment is the explicit assurance that neither those saved, nor those condemned had any conception that they were dealing with a religious issue at all. 'Lord when saw we thee an-hungered?' " What happens in union elections, board rooms, council and cabinet meetings, ultimately determines the quality of life people enjoy. It determines who becomes rich and who starves, who gets justice, and whether as a country we shall sink or swim.

Some ministers feeling keenly this failure on the part of the laity to represent Christ in the world, to be salt and leaven, to become politically and socially involved, have themselves increasingly become the front-line troops.

Although I am against there being a sharp line of demarcation between clergy and laity, I am not opposed to a reasonable division of labour. I would not like to see the minister's role redefined in such a way that his *primary* preoccupation became direct participation in social or political action, rather than the ministry of word and sacrament. When worship is meaningful and relevant, it can be for many, a 'time of awareness', making them more sensitive to the 'God in their midst', to the Christ in the hungry, the naked and the homeless.

In the time of Jesus, bread occupied a central place in Jewish thought. Palestine was a land plagued with drought. The pressure of hunger was never far from the Jews. It was after Jesus had been for some time without food that the reality of the temptation to spend his life meeting men's physical needs came home to him. "Look at this business of being hungry. Why don't you dedicate your life to meeting that kind of need, giving people what they really want. After all they are not much better than animals. Fill their stomachs and they will make you a king." But Jesus refused to accept this devilish analysis as a solution of the human dilemma. He knew that even if all man's food problems were removed and the future was made financially secure, there would remain a hunger more clamant still. Zaccheus the wealthy publican had plenty of food but an emptiness in his heart. Full barns may satisfy cattle, but not man himself. "Is not life more than food and the body than clothing?"

When Arnold Toynbee was asked who were the greatest benefactors of mankind, he did not choose the inventor of the car or the aeroplane. Nor did he speak of those who discovered the secrets of electricity, radio or television. He replied, "Confucius, the Buddha, Socrates, the prophets of Israel and Jesus." He chose them because they all sought in their own day to shed light on the really big questions of life, questions about life's meaning and purpose. When Washington University in St Louis celebrated its centenary, the committee responsible for the celebrations was headed by Sir Arthur Compton, a Nobel prize-winning physicist. It was assumed that because of this, many leading scientists would be invited to share in the celebrations. But the committee decided otherwise. They issued the following statement. "The university is inviting speakers who will consider such questions as, 'Can life as a whole be said to have meaning and purpose?' 'What things are most worth believing and hoping?' 'What values deserve our supreme allegiance?'"

Jesus refused to confine his role to that of doctor or social worker. He had a gospel to proclaim. Though attuned to man's need for bread, he was also attuned to man's deeper hunger for love, meaning, freedom, worth and, deepest hunger of all, for God. He was 'the man for others', but first and foremost 'the man for God'. If the Church is to be faithful to her Lord, she can never be content with a gospel of social betterment and material help.

Abraham Lincoln said, "The sources of power in this nation are not so much with those who shape its laws, as with those who shape its public opinion." Our world faces a prodigious choice. Whose ideas will shape public opinion, those of Christ or Marx or *Playboy*? In our day unbelief has sudden⸗

become a booming chorus. Through the mass media a vocal minority, self-styled avant-garde, boldly proclaim their godless philosophies and new morality. Desperately concerned about the outcome of this battle for the mind of man, and the shaping of the values of our society, I believe it is a minister's prime responsibility to share with people, by means of preaching, group discussion and visiting, the eternal truths of the Christian faith. He can thus not only strengthen the faith of his members, but enable them better to champion Christian beliefs and values in a world that is calling them in question.

The clergy ought to be open to the content of other disciplines. 'What does he know of scripture who only scripture knows?' Ministers can learn a great deal from psychology and sociology, but there is much more to the ministry than can be defined in social, political or psychological terms. It is just not true that a form of Christianity that has no 'God-talk', or 'ought-talk' will attract modern man. When Winston Churchill learned during a visit to Edinburgh that the Rev. Dr George Gunn preached each Sunday to over five hundred people, he said, "If I were to speak twice a Sunday in the same place to the same people on my own subject, politics, at the end of six months there would be no one there to listen to me." Karl Barth, one of the greatest theological minds of the twentieth century, preached one summer in a church near to his home. What fascinated him was that despite the fact that he was not gifted in communicating with the ordinary man, people kept coming back. This caused him to examine what it was about the Bible and worship that attracted them. The majority came to church secretly hoping that some light might be shed on the mystery of life and that they might receive power for the mastery of life. The Church that neglects the teaching ministry or minimises the importance of worship is digging its own grave.

Though there is no essential difference between the clergy and laity, there are good practical reasons for some kind of division of labour within the 'team' ministry. Many of the problems and failures of the Church in our day stem from the fact that for far too long both clergy and laity have neglected their special functions and responsibilities.

CHAPTER EIGHTEEN

DOUBTS ABOUT OUR ROLE IN LIFE

Once upon a time a king commanded his favourite minstrel to compose a song which the minstrel could sing without ceasing. Perpetual music was thus to be installed in the royal palace. Aware that to fail the commission would mean his execution, the minstrel tried to keep his head! He strummed a few chords and then said, "Sire, if I must sing a song that goes on forever, I will sing about the creation of our glorious country." The song began,

> A bird flew to a distant strand
> And picked up there a grain of sand
> And returning to our land
> He dropped it.

The second verse went like the first and so on. At first the king enjoyed hearing the attractive voice of his favourite singer, but as the verses continued in mindless repetition, he thundered, "Stop it! Such endless nonsense drives me mad."

That is fiction, but it is fact that the routine of life gets many down, each tomorrow a re-enactment of today.

> "The sun gets up, the sun goes down
> The hands on the clock go round and round"

until we want to cry, "Stop it! Such nonsense is maddening Assembly lines and mass production have certainly raised standard of living, but they have aggravated the monoton doing the same thing over and over again. The routine wou more tolerable if what we did seemed relevant to a meaningful universe, but many doubt whether work has an beyond the immediate financial reward.

Lucy says to Charlie Brown, "The trouble with yc you don't understand the meaning of life." How man

Browns there are, people for whom life is a riddle with no key.
This identity crisis was highlighted in a cartoon depicting a
learned professor taking part in the television programme,
'Mastermind'. His specialist subject was the history of
philosophy. Having answered difficult factual questions, he was
finally asked, "What is the meaning of life?" "Pass," he
replied. In *Death of a Salesman*, Biff, one of Willy Loman's
sons, pondering his father's tragic life, says, "The trouble with
Dad was that he never knew who he was." His frantic attempts
to cover his spiritual nakedness with the rags of public
recognition had been to no avail. He plaintively kept telling his
family, "I'm well known. I'm well liked." But all the time there
was the desolating sense of emptiness within.

In our day meaninglessness threatens to destroy much that
is fine in individuals and communities. Meaning is the central
problem of existence. Does life add up to anything? Does the
bottom line show red or black? Such questions are not merely
interesting subjects for philosophical study. They concern most
people at some stage of their lives. Recall those wild cartoons
which most children enjoy. Every now and then an animated
character runs unknowingly off the edge of a cliff. He keeps on
running in empty air until he looks down and sees that there is
nothing under his feet. Then he crashes screaming and terror-
stricken to a temporary cartoon death. Are we not all cartoon
characters in mid-air? So long as we don't look down we can
keep on running. But there comes the moment of truth when we
suddenly become aware of the awful void beneath us, of what
the writer of Ecclesiastes called "the emptiness of all endeavour".

> Emptiness, all is empty... What does man gain from all his labour
> and his toil here under the sun? Generations come and generations
> go, while the earth endures forever.
> The sun rises and the sun goes down; back it returns to its place and
> rises there again. The wind blows south, the wind blows north, round
> and round it goes and returns full circle. All streams run into the sea,
> yet the sea never overflows; back to the place from which the streams
> ran they return to run again.
> All things are wearisome; no man can speak of them all... What has
> happened will happen again, and what has been done will be done
> again, and there is nothing new under the sun... I have seen all the
> deeds which are done here under the sun; they are all emptiness and
> chasing the wind. (Eccl. 1:2ff., N.E.B)

From first-hand experience the writer of Ecclesiastes speaks of the awful void, the emptiness inherent in many of his achievements and in many of the pleasures he had craved as a young man. Having got what he wanted, he no longer wanted it. Treasure chests had become vanity boxes.

> I undertook great works; I built myself houses and planted vineyards; I made myself gardens and parks... I bought slaves, male and female... I had possessions, more cattle and flocks than any of my predecessors in Jerusalem; I amassed silver and gold also, the treasures of kings and provinces; I acquired singers, men and women, and all that man delights in... Whatever my eyes coveted I refused them nothing, nor did I deny myself any pleasure... Then I turned and reviewed all my handiwork, all my labour and toil, and I saw that everything was emptiness and chasing the wind, of no profit under the sun. (Eccl. 2:4-II, N.E.B.)

We live today in a very different age, in a civilisation equipped with the glittering machinery of technology. Our pace of living is much quicker, yet many would rise to second the motion of the Old Testament writer that life is nothing more than a gigantic shaggy-dog story, a sick cosmic joke. The playwright Samuel Beckett says, "This is the void at the heart of poor electronically affluent man, the gnawing empty feeling that nothing makes sense" Another author when asked to describe a typical modern person chose to describe a medical officer of health carrying on his weary struggle against bad housing, overcrowding and venereal desease, and finding his greatest enemy to be his own heart's deep insistent doubt as to whether the whole effort was worthwhile.

The astronomical number of tranquillisers and the vast amount of alcohol we consume as a nation are further indications of the burden of futility, insecurity and boredom which hang over a great deal of our contemporary life. Some seek to dispel the boredom by going from job to job, wife to wife, house to house, new sensation to new sensation, but more often than not they simply become more jaded. It was so with the Samaritan woman at the well, the one who, having had five husbands, was living with a man who was not her husband. Her jadedness was painfully obvious to Jesus.

The phrase 'under the sun' which the writer of Ecclesiastes uses means 'without God'. Just as there is a flatness about a two-dimensional photograph of a three-dimensional scene, so there is an awful boredom and futility about the daily routine when looked at simply 'under the sun', without any divine reference. If we are alone in a meaningless world, if traditional moral and spiritual values are without cosmic support, if we are accountable to nothing beyond the whim of the moment, then the temptation is strong to do whatever will break the routine, whatever will provide kicks. In moments of depression the temptation is also strong to ask, "What is the point of working hard? What is the point of life itself?" Here we have the root cause of the marked increase in suicides, vandalism and absenteeism. The ultimate enemy in life is not pain or physical hardship but the feeling that what we do does not matter, that we are not important.

Many exclude God from their thinking and from the thousand little things that made up yesterday and from the thousand yesterdays and todays that make up life. It is not surprising that they then fail to find meaning and purpose in life, that they live in the pseudo-faith that we are simply children with chance for our heritage and luck for our destiny. Since the sickness is spiritual, the healing must be religious. Pills and alcohol are no lasting solution. Providing at best a temporary palliative they often introduce other problems and difficulties. Only a religious outlook on life can provide the meaning without which there can be no healing. But many dismiss as mediaeval or irrelevant anything to do with religion. The description of a philosopher as a person in a dark cellar looking for a black cat is usually greeted with applause, for many doubt that life has meaning. The applause usually increases when it is added that a theologian is a person who claims to have found it. Despite the mocking applause, I believe that in the life and teaching of Jesus the meaning of life has been revealed. Because of his coming into the world we know that man is much more than an ape who has learned to shave, more than an ingenious assembly of portable plumbing, more than a shuttlecock of circumstance getting battered backwards and forwards. Jesus reminded his contemporaries that human life, far from being framed by a maternity ward and a cemetery, or by two great silences, is lived ut against the backdrop of eternity. He thus helped heal many of their self-despisings. He reminded them that though they might never be famous, the contribution they could make with their one or two talents was of cosmic importance. Just as God creates the glory of the Scottish hills in autumn out of billions of tiny little heather bells, so out of billions of thoughtful words and ordinary acts of service, done in an uncommon spirit, God hopes to create a finer world.

Jesus also taught that all that we have and are is God's gift to us. Whatever our talents are, we did nothing to deserve them. We speak of certain people being gifted but seldom ask—gifted by whom or gifted for what? "What do you possess that was not given you? If then you really received it all as a gift, why take the credit to yourself?" Our role in life is that of steward. The steward was the forerunner of the factor or manager. Wealthy landowners employed stewards to supervise and manage their money, farms or vineyards. There were two significant characteristics of the steward's role. Firstly, he owned none of the things over which he had control. His role was to manage them in the interests of the owner, not in his own interests. Secondly, he was answerable to the owner for what he did with what had been entrusted to him.

Everything we inherit has a little tag attached, 'in trust'; everything is to be used in God's interests which are the interests of the great human family. If anything is clear in the Bible it is that God wants us to subordinate the 'Big I', with its shrill claim for priority, its constant preoccupation with 'me' and 'mine', 'my kingdom come, my will be done', and ask instead at each stage of life, "What would Jesus have me do?" What we are is God's gift to us. What we do with it is our gift to God. How well Fritz Kreisler illustrates this understanding of life.

> I was born with music in my soul. People do not seem to understand just why I do not feel that I have any right to spend my money carelessly. It is very simple. I feel that I am a steward of both my talent and the money that comes to me from that talent. It is God's gift and I am its steward.

Dietrich Bonhoeffer in his poem 'Who am I?' composed in a Nazi concentration camp, ends with the lines, "Whoever I am, thou knowest O God I am thine." It was this faith that, thoug' our lives may be brief, we are a God-loved people in a God-loved world, and that though our grasp on God may be weak, his grasp of us is strong, that kept Bonhoeffer serene when finally taken out and shot by a German firing squad.

It really is time that we stopped apologising for the Christian understanding of life. As Berdyaev said, "Life in time remains without meaning if it does not receive its meaning from eternity."

It is also time we stopped apologising for the Christian way of life. Life must have a larger purpose than the pampering of our bodies and the accumulation of grown-up toys, or else it is not life at all. Lord Byron wrote about 'high society' in the London of his day: "Society is now one polished horde, formed of two mighty tribes — the Bores and the Bored." No doubt that was unfair. But these two classes do describe accurately people who are all wrapped up in themselves. As soon as a person ceases to have a commitment which he deems worth while, the self begins to disintegrate. Ours is a world where a great deal that is wrong is wrong because people live self-centred lives, refuse to share and care, to give and forgive. As we are thrown more closely together, as the points of friction between individuals and nations multiply, an increase in brotherly love and concern becomes a stark necessity, rather than just a desirable option. If asked who most curse human life, I would reply those who give free reign to their aggresive and demanding natures, dictators in the home, office, factory or nation who are concerned only with their own advancement and with getting their own way. If asked who most enrich life, I would point to those who stand resolutely by that caring view of life which seeks to turn inequality into an opportunity for creating that human fellowship and brotherhood which service alone can create. Those who have learned to care are those least in need of proof that life makes sense.

Writing to a friend, Mother Teresa said, "Use the beautiful gift God has given you for His greater glory. All that you have and all that you are and all that you can be and do, let it all be for Him and Him alone." To reflect the love of God into e lives of others, to do something beautiful for God with the ts entrusted to us, that is our role in life.

CHAPTER NINETEEN
DOUBTS ABOUT DEATH

The capacity to think about death, the one inescapable fact of existence, is as far as we know, a capacity which only human beings have. Yet how unwilling many are to exercise it. A conspiracy of silence surrounds death. With regard to death we are like children who when they see ahead of them something that frightens them or that they don't want to see, clap their hands over their eyes to shut out the sight. They are quite happy as long as they cannot see it.

The fact that today many die, not at home, but in hospitals or in special homes for the terminally ill, and that when they die their bodies are taken direct to the funeral parlour, makes it easier for people to avoid close contact with death. In many parts of Scotland the process of dying is more remote than in former generations. In a village a hundred years ago when someone was dying everyone knew about it, even the children. They heard the last words and watched the breathing stop and the body lose its colour. Then very often one or two of the family prepared the body for the coffin. On the day of the funeral the coffin was carried to the grave by close friends and buried in a grave which often the deceased had previously purchased in anticipation of his own death.

Dr Steere tells of a Norwegian peasant who in the autumn before the roads became impassable had his son purchase and bring home a wooden coffin in case he might die that winter. Many today would regard that as morbid, yet I am sure that the old Norwegian whose simple philosophy of life was, "By God's grace I am going to live until I die and then I am going to live forever", would have had difficulty in understanding a society which deals in such elaborate concealment of death.

Martin Heidegger once observed that human beings have a

facility for retreating from the mysterious to the manageable. They are embarrassed to talk about holy things like God, love and death. We cannot capture God but we can lose ourselves in religion and we do. We cannot fathom real love, so we reduce it to romance or sex and talk about it sentimentally or clinically. We cannot handle death but we can keep ourselves busy with funeral arrangements and we do.

To avoid speaking about death we use all kinds of euphemisms, like 'passing away' and 'falling asleep'. We use the words 'if anything happens to me'. In America, funeral homes have become cosmetic parlours attempting to make death as much like life as possible. Here in Britain, family and friends often play the futile game of pretending that the dying person is not dying. They keep assuring him he is looking much better and will soon be back on his feet. It is considered hopelessly bad manners for any bedside visitor to mention death. Some hospital doctors have a high level of anxiety about death. Their goal is the promotion of life, which occasionally means little more than the prolongation of existence. Death, being equated with failure, is to be staved off at all costs.

I read somewhere how in India the fakirs used to sit beside pools of water with piles of coloured dust beside them. They had perfected the art of dropping the dust so skilfully upon the still surface of the pool that they could make recognisable portraits of distinguished people. Then the breeze would ruffle the pool and the picture would disappear. Is that how it is with God? Does he take coloured dust and drop it on life's water and, behold, Socrates, or Moses or Jesus come into being. And then does the breeze disturb the water so that they disappear? One moment a loved one is with us, light in his eyes, speech on his lips, strength in his hands. Then a moment later he is gone. Gone forever, is that how it is? Do darkness and death have the last word? If so then understandably we avoid talking about death and seek at all costs to prolong our life-span. More difficult to understand is the reluctance to speak about death of those who profess to believe that life does not end with death and that those who die are setting out on a glorious adventure. Is this reluctance an indication that many who profess to believe in 'the life everlasting' secretly have doubts whether 'death is swallowed up in victory'? In bondage to the visible and the tangible many today wonder whether anything lives on when the body dies, whether belief in the resurrection is anything more than wishful thinking.

The 20th century Church has too often failed her members by not stressing sufficiently that in this world it is the invisible which is most real, that the creative realities with which they inwardly deal and by which they live are for the most part unseen. The 13th century cathedral of which I am minister is gloriously visible; not visible however are the spiritual needs it was built to meet, or the faiths expressed in it, or the skill of the builders and masons who planned and erected it. Those who have seen people completely transformed by having a new idea or insight or thought take hold of them are left in no doubt as to the power of invisible, intangible ideas and insights. We all value the outward expressions of love, but love itself we have never seen. Nor have we seen hope, yet what is life without hope? Any visitor to Calcutta can see the face of Mother Teresa engraved with the love and sorrow of a life totally dedicated to Christ, but they cannot physically see the faith that impels and undergirds her.

Reacting against the sentimental pietism which dreamt of heaven and neglected earth, which understressed the importance of the secular and the social, the Church has recently been guilty of understressing the mystical and eternal dimensions that there are to life. Marxist jibes about religion being the opium of the people, or about pie-in-the-sky by-and-by, have made many Church members hesitant to speak about the hope of heaven. It is not however sufficient that the Church should call on people to make the world a better place. If man is only dust, albeit intelligent dust, is it worth his while to 'make a better world' of dust? Are we nothing more than fertiliser for some future Utopia?

The Church believes we are much more than that, that our being here means something and means something portentous and eternal, that the human soul is the one inconceivably precious thing. Part of the calling of the Church is to help people see life against the backdrop of eternity, to help them reach a philosophy of life that will include a philosophy of death.

Taking death seriously can change the evaluation people set on many things in life. "So teach us to number our days that we may apply our hearts unto wisdom", said the Psalmist. The writer of Ecclesiastes also felt there was more to be learned in the house of mourning than in the house of feasting.

When Charles Wertenbaker, the editor of 'Time' magazine, learned that he had a cancerous growth, he decided to swim out into the ocean near his home, look back and remember for the last time, and then fill his lungs with water. "The alternative," he said, "was hospitals, pain, becoming a patient instead of a person, reduced to something less than a man." But fortunately he changed his mind. Having suffered little physical pain during his life, he felt it would be cowardly to avoid it now. An exploratory operation revealed he had only three months to live. Against the judgment of his doctors, Wertenbaker went home to die. As the family faced the truth themselves they also revealed it to many of their friends and neighbours. His son taught him how to play the guitar. He began to write a book about living and dying. He found greater appreciation of daily experiences, the sound of Bach, the feel of the sand and the wind. He looked inward, reviewing and evaluating himself and his relations with others. He looked outward and his love ripened. Near the end, glad that he had not taken that swim in the ocean, he wrote, "I'd have drowned the best part of my life." Charles Wertenbaker died. He did not just fade away.

Though people often try to be nonchalant about death, when death touches someone near and dear to them, it is different. Few can contemplate the death of a loved one and say with a shrug of the shoulders, "I do not care whether that is the end of her or not." When Charles Williams died, C.S. Lewis wrote to his friend Owen Barfield,

> "This, the first really serious loss I have suffered, has given corroboration to my belief in immortality such as I never dreamed of... To put it in a nutshell, what the idea of death has done to him is nothing to what he has done to the idea of death. Hit it for six."

Often at funeral services I have been led to wonder what is going on in the minds of the mourners, some of whom will never be in church again until they return on a similar occasion.

Some are obviously made uncomfortable by being in the presence of death and in the precincts of religion, and by hearing the minister say the awesome words, "This mortal body must put on immortality"; yet deep down few would have it any other way, and they would be in no other place.

The death of the body is no more strange than the death of a pair of shoes. Both were meant to serve a given purpose. Both finally wear out. Fortunately we are not contained between our hats and boots, or chained to our hearts and livers. Benjamin Franklin was aware of this when he wrote his own epitaph.

> The Body of Benjamin Franklin, printer
> (Like the Cover of an old book
> Its contents worn out
> And stript of its lettering and gilding)
> Lies here, food for worms!
> But the work itself shall not be lost
> For it will, as he believed, appear once more
> In a new and more beautiful edition
> Corrected and amended
> By its Author.

Concerning the nature of life after death, people ask many unanswerable questions. "What will our loved ones look like?" "What about the stillborn child I had?" "Will he be in heaven?" "Will he be recognisable?..." People are often surprised and disappointed when to many of these questions a minister replies, "I don't know." I take comfort from the fact that the details of life after death are in far better hands than mine. God who invented friendship, compassion, warmth and love will take care of these details. I am certain also that life in heaven will be richer than this life just as this life is richer than life in the womb. Dr Fosdick in one of his books asks us to imagine two unborn babies, conversing about the prospect that lies ahead of them. Says one: "Leaving this womb can mean nothing but death. We are absolutely dependent on this matrix which sustains us and feeds us." Says the other: "But nature has been developing us for nine months. Nature is not utterly irrational. She is preparing us for something." Answers the unbelieving baby: "Describe if you can the kind of world you think we are going to be born into. What is it like?" That of course would completely stump the believing babe. "I can' describe it," he replies. "I have no idea what it is like. But I am sure nature would never do what she has been doing all these months with no meaning or purpose in the process." To which the unbelieving babe answers with scorn: "That is blind faith." But the believing babe was right!

St Paul likens the glory of eternal life to seeds and ripened plants. We hold some grain seed in our hands, little spheres of vegetable matter. If we give them to a scientist for examination, he will give us a report as to their physical characteristics–size, weight, colour, chemical analysis and the rest. Yet any child would know on reading the report that the most important thing has been omitted, and that is, what the seed will produce. There are obvious differences between the seed and the ripened plants, and yet there is also continuity from the death of the seed to the life and maturity of the grain. An Eskimo who had never seen fully grown grain would have difficulty believing that from these little seeds, a fraction of an inch across, there would come a waving grain field. How much more difficult to comprehend, let alone describe, the nature of the new 'spiritual body' God will give us.

There is, however, shadow as well as light in the biblical picture of life beyond death. "Whoever speaks of immortality and does not immediately mention the Judgment is himself in danger of the Judgment," wrote Sören Kierkegaard. Jokes about the last judgment are numerous because the reality of that judgment refuses to leave us alone. Those reared in conservative churches often have a spine-chilling picture of the final judgment, a picture of people standing before God seated on a great white throne. According to this picture the Supreme Judge holds in his hands the book which records every good and bad thing they have ever done. Each person stands there with knees knocking as the celestial computer totals the score of their earthly record. Then a voice like the thunder of waters pronounces a verdict, sentencing the individual to the torments of an eternal hell or admitting them to eternal bliss. Of King Nebuchadnezzar it was said, "Whom he would he slew, and whom he would he kept alive." The conception of God as a divine Nebuchadnezzar, who in his wrath sends to hell all who ɔ not bear the name Christian (all non-union members!) and all who have not achieved merit badges in this life–a concept so vividly portrayed by Michelangelo and Dante and Milton–is, I believe, false, because it is out of character with the God made known to the world in Jesus, a God who waits patiently for the prodigal to come home, who goes out looking for the lost sheep and does not rest until he finds it.

Equally mistaken is the sentimental picture which others have of a world from which any notion of ultimate judgment is missing. Few would want to live in such a world, a world where it did not matter whether we live like a Nero or a Paul, a Hitler or a Schweitzer, a Stalin or a Sakharov. Something within us hungers to believe that one deed is better than another, that there are qualitative distinctions between human actions. God's wrath, as the New Testament understands it, is not a capricious anger. It is enmity towards all that spoils the life of God's children, all that perverts, destroys or injures God's beloved creation.

The doctrine of 'wholly unmerited grace', that we are justified by faith, not good works, that God loves us in spite of what we are, not because of what we are, is one of the great Christian doctrines. It has, however, so often been misunderstood, giving the false impression that in the last resort human behaviour is unimportant, that Berdyaev maintained that this doctrine has in fact been one of the major causes of "the demonic materialism of Western culture". If it is not possible by our deeds to lay up some treasure in heaven, then people are very likely to lay up a lot on earth.

The Biblical emphasis is two-fold. It stresses that God is willing to receive us as we are, but it also stresses the need to put ourselves at God's disposal so that he can perform 'good works' through us, those acts of kindness and love which are 'the best portion of a good man's life'. (Compare Matthew 25 v 31f and James 2 v 14f) God is concerned about what we do with our lives and talents. It does matter to him whether we live self-centred or compassionate lives.

In the New Testament, life and death are set over against each other. To be alive means to be alive to God, and to the fellowship of other people. It is to have entered upon a life that has a caring and eternal quality about it. To be dead is to allow self-centredness and lovelessness to separate us from God and our fellow human beings. In one of his parables Jesus likens heaven to a party. Everyone is invited by a host who goes to endless trouble to find guests. The word 'judgment' dramatises the difference between accepting or declining the invitation, coming inside or staying outside. Heaven is to relate. Hell is to withdraw. Berdyaev spoke of 'each man's right to Hell', each man's right to decline the invitation, to exclude himself, preferring to be isolated in self-love.

In a B.B.C. documentary on casinos, a lady croupier, married with a little son, confessed that she had reached the stage when babies and gardens no longer had any appeal. Working night after night in the superficial, acquisitive atmosphere of the casino had blinded her to the wonder of many of life's most precious things. Sadder still was the fact that she had no desire to change. Is it not similarly so with those for whom self is the perspective from which all is viewed, the norm by which all is measured, the focal point round which all is organised? Interested only in what is to their own advantage or in what contributes to their own pleasure, they become more and more incapable of being at home in a spiritually sensitive world, a world characterised by caring love. Those filled with hate or bitterness and those primarily concerned with status would be as ill at ease in Heaven as a compulsive gambler in a community where no one else wanted to gamble. Heaven would be hell for them.

God will never stop loving us. That is the good news of Christianity. It is also the essential message of the parable of the prodigal son. Whenever our feet turn homeward the welcome is there. But what if we refuse to turn, or have no desire to go to the party? This was the question that disturbed the gentle Quaker John Whittier.

> Forever round the Mercy Seat
> The guiding lights of love shall burn
> But what if habit bound, thy feet
> Shall lack the will to turn?